TREASURY OF

MW01243198

Language Handbook
Grade 4

Printed in the United States of America

ISBN 0-15-304868-9

13 073 98

THIS BOOK IS PRINTED ON **ACID-FREE, RECYCLED PAPER.** ⊛

HARCOURT BRACE & COMPANY
ORLANDO · ATLANTA · AUSTIN · BOSTON · SAN FRANCISCO · CHICAGO · DALLAS · NEW YORK ·
TORONTO · LONDON

Contents

WRITING FORMS

GRAMMAR, USAGE, & MECHANICS

HANDWRITING

ADDITIONAL PRACTICE

Using the Handbook

What's the first thing you do when you pick up a new magazine or book? You flip through it to see what captures your interest. Try doing that now. What kinds of things does this handbook include? What do you think you can use it for?

WHAT IS A HANDBOOK?

A handbook is like a toolbox. It contains the tools you need to do different tasks. In this handbook, the tools are language.

Use this language handbook as a quick reference to all kinds of helpful tips for writing, speaking, and listening. You will find

- ☑ **tips to help you start writing.**
- ☑ **information about writing forms.**
- ☑ **handwriting models and hints.**
- ☑ **easy-to-understand rules of grammar.**
- ☑ **practice with language.**

Use the information in this handbook as you would use tools.

SECTIONS OF THE HANDBOOK

This handbook has five sections. Four of the sections include information about writing, writing forms, grammar, and handwriting. The fifth section provides practice with language.

WRITING

This section includes all the information you need to plan, write, and polish your writing.

WRITING FORMS

This section provides you with models for writing stories, poems, how-to paragraphs — and more.

GRAMMAR, USAGE, AND MECHANICS

In this section, you will find easy-to-read information about parts of speech, sentences, and punctuation.

HANDWRITING

This section includes suggestions for making your handwriting clear for your readers.

ADDITIONAL PRACTICE

Practice exercises in this section help you master the rules of grammar, usage, and mechanics.

Use the sections of this book as you would a toolbox that has different sections for tools.

HOW TO FIND INFORMATION IN THE HANDBOOK

Suppose your teacher gives you a writing assignment and you are unsure what to do. Use this handbook as a reference tool to help you find the answers to your questions. Two of the best ways to find information in this book are to use the table of contents and the index.

- The **table of contents** follows the title page, or first page, of this book. It tells you the main sections of this book and the pages on which they begin. Use it when you want to find main topics quickly.

- The **index** appears at the back of the book. It lists every topic in this book and the pages on which the information appears. Topics are listed in alphabetical order so that you can find them quickly.

BONUS

Each section also has its own mini-table of contents!

Perfect!

Writing

The Writing Process

In writing, you can use a plan called the *writing process* to help you think of ideas and then write about them. Here are the steps of the writing process.

PREWRITING

Identify your TAP— task, audience, and purpose. Then choose a topic. Gather and organize information about the topic.

DRAFTING

Put your ideas in writing. Don't worry about making mistakes. You can fix them later.

RESPONDING AND REVISING

Reread your writing to see if it meets your purpose. Meet with a partner or in a group to discuss and revise it.

PROOFREADING

Correct spelling, grammar, usage, mechanics, and capitalization errors.

PUBLISHING

Share your writing. Decide how you want to publish your work.

The writing process helps you move back and forth between stages of your writing.

Planning Tips

Did you know you begin writing the moment you start thinking about doing it? Here are some things you can do to help you plan and organize your thinking and writing.

UNDERSTANDING TASK, AUDIENCE, AND PURPOSE

Before you begin writing, it is a good idea to decide your task, audience, and purpose (TAP). Ask yourself these questions:

Task

- **What am I writing?**

  Do I want to write a letter, a poem, or something else?

Audience

- **For whom am I writing?**

  Am I writing for my teacher, a younger child, a friend, myself, or someone else?

Purpose

- **Why am I writing?**

  Am I writing to persuade someone, to give information, or for another reason?

What is your TAP?

GATHERING IDEAS

You never have to feel "stuck" when it's time to think of ideas for writing. Ideas can come from many places. Here are different ways to gather ideas.

Where do you get your ideas?

- Look through your journal.

- Make a list of ideas. Don't worry about the order. You can organize your ideas later.

- Brainstorm with a friend or in a group.

- Freewrite. This means just start writing and don't stop.

- Look in your portfolio for ideas.

- Use the questions news reporters ask to help them write information. Ask yourself *Who? What? When? Where? Why?* and *How?*

- Read for writing. Look through favorite books and magazines for ideas.

- Use graphic organizers. Make a chart or web to help you gather ideas.

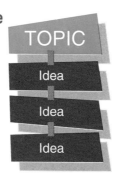

An **inverted triangle** is another useful graphic organizer. Use it when you want to narrow a topic that is too broad.

General Topic

Smaller Topic

Topic to Write About

Graphic organizers help you brainstorm ideas.

Use a **star** graphic organizer for descriptive writing. Brainstorm words and ideas that appeal to the five senses.

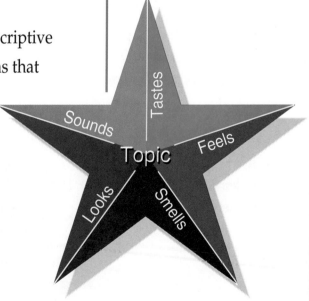

Sounds
Tastes
Feels
Topic
Looks
Smells

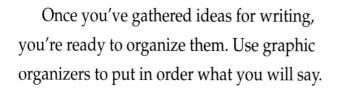

ORGANIZING INFORMATION

Once you've gathered ideas for writing, you're ready to organize them. Use graphic organizers to put in order what you will say.

A **time line** helps you put events in sequence, or time order. You can use one to help you write a story, a history report, or a sketch of someone's life.

Graphic organizers also help you put your ideas in order.

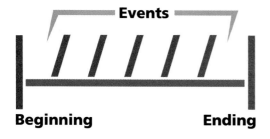

Events

Beginning   **Ending**

A **story map** helps you plan a story.

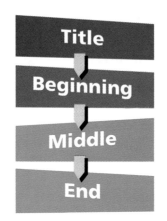

Title

Beginning

Middle

End

A **Venn diagram** is useful when you want to compare or contrast. It helps you tell what is alike and different about people, places, or things.

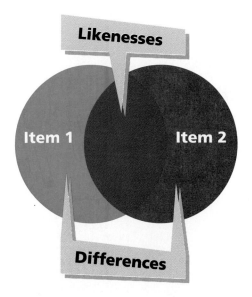

Use the graphic organizer that works best for your TAP.

A **how-to chart** helps you organize a how-to paragraph or steps for directions. Write any materials needed. Then list the steps in order.

How to_____

Materials_____
_____
_____

Step 1_____

Step 2_____

Step 3_____

An **outline** helps you group information and put it in order. Use an outline to organize notes for a research report.

Topic
I. Main Idea
A. Detail
B. Detail
C. Detail
II. Main Idea
A. Detail
B. Detail
C. Detail

Outlines are great for organizing essays, history reports, and science reports!

Writing Tips

Getting started can sometimes seem like the hardest part of writing. However, it doesn't have to be. Remember that you can change what you write at any time. One of the best tips for writing is just to start writing. You can make corrections later.

To relax, imagine that you are writing to a friend.

GETTING STARTED

If you're having trouble even starting your writing, you don't have to start at the beginning. Start in the middle or even at the end. Go back later and add the beginning! Here are some other tips to help you get started:

- **If you're nervous, try to relax. Imagine that you're writing to a friend.**

- **Change your writing method. Print or use a computer instead of writing out words.**

- **Picture a scene. Then scribble or draw it.**

- **Freewrite until you're comfortable.**

- **Use your notes!**

DRAFTING STRATEGIES

WRITING A GOOD BEGINNING

A good beginning in an essay or a report tells readers right away what the writing is about. Whenever possible, your beginning should grab the readers' attention and make them want to read more. Here are some ways to help you write an interesting beginning:

- **State your main idea, explaining why your readers should care about it.**

- **Ask a question that makes your readers think.**

- **State interesting or unusual facts.**

WRITING A GOOD ENDING

A good ending wraps up all the ideas presented in a piece of writing. Here are some tips for writing a good ending:

- **Restate the main idea in a different way.**

- **Summarize the main points covered.**

- **Challenge your readers to take action.**

Don't make your readers guess what they're reading about!

Polishing Your Writing

When you polish writing, you are **revising,** or editing, it to make it better. *Revising* means

- **Adding**—inserting words, sentences, or paragraphs
- **Cutting**—taking out repeated or unrelated information
- **Replacing**—crossing out information and putting new information in its place
- **Moving**—rearranging information so that it's in a better order

REVISING CONFERENCES

One good way to revise is to get someone else's opinion. Work with one or more partners. Others can offer good ideas to improve your writing. When you work with a partner, remember to

- be positive and polite;
- ask questions rather than criticize;
- work together to get the best results.

Editor's Marks

$\wedge$ Add something.

$\wp$ Cut something.

$\wedge$ Replace something.

$\mathcal{O}$ Move something.

Revising Checklist

☑ **Does my topic sentence tell the main idea?**

☑ **Do my detail sentences support my topic sentence?**

☑ **Does the order make sense?**

☑ **Are my sentences clear?**

You can make your writing more interesting by expanding and combining sentences. Expand sentences by adding details and examples that make a vivid word picture.

Use a variety of sentences in your writing.

eagerly *of this special day*
Juan ˄awaited the dawn˄.

You can join two sentences with words such as *and*, *or*, or *but*, called *conjunctions*. Use a comma before the conjunction.

but
It was sunny. ˄It was cool.

You can also combine sentences that have the same subject or predicate, or adjectives describing the same subject:

Juan stretched out his arms.
and
Juan˄ took a deep breath.

and *were*
Juan ˄was glad. Mo ˄was glad.

Mo was happy. Mo was jumpy,
and
Mo was playful.

23

USING FIGURATIVE LANGUAGE

Help your writing come alive by using comparisons. Comparisons help your readers see things in a new way. Similes and metaphors are two kinds of comparisons.

Create word pictures by comparing two things.

Similes

- **A simile compares two unlike objects using the word *like* or *as*:**

Juan was *as* excited *as* a puppy.

Juan was *like* an excited puppy.

Try to complete these similes to help your readers visualize something.

The breeze was as gentle as _____.

The surface of the water sparkled like _____.

Metaphors

- **A metaphor compares two unlike objects by suggesting that one thing *is* another:**

 The sun is a bright spotlight in the sky.

Imagine something to compare these items to:

    clouds   stream   trees

EDITING WORDY SENTENCES

Good writers avoid wordy language. Try to say what you mean in as few words as possible. When you revise, cross out words that don't add to the meaning.

Mo ~~made an attempt~~ *tried* to jump out of the boat ~~they were in~~.

The words *made an attempt* were replaced with one word, *tried.* The words *they were in* were cut because they add nothing. The revised sentence has the same meaning, but it's easier to read.

USING VIVID WORDS

Don't bore your readers. Use specific nouns and vivid verbs. Check a dictionary or thesaurus. Look at the difference two word changes can make!

The ~~person~~ *fisher* had caught a ~~fish~~ *whopper!*

Choose vivid words to make your writing sparkle!

RESPONDING AND REVISING STRATEGIES

PROOFREADING TIPS

Are you ready to publish your work after revising it? Not quite. You still have to proofread it. Proofreading is different from revising. It is a separate step in which you check for errors in spelling, grammar, usage, and mechanics. Here are some tips to help you proofread:

- Keep a dictionary nearby to check spelling.
- Read your writing aloud to find mistakes, such as words left out.
- Cover up the rest of the paper as you read each line to check for errors.
- Check the overall appearance for neatness.
- If your work is handwritten, be sure it is clear and easy to read.

- Check for sentence fragments by reading each sentence word for word.
- If you're not sure something is correct, look it up in the grammar section of this handbook.
- Use proofreader's marks to show the changes you want to make.

Proofreader's Marks

Mark	Meaning
☰	Capitalize.
⊙	Add a period.
∧	Add something.
⋏	Add a comma.
⩔⩔	Add quotation marks.
⩘	Cut something.
⌃	Replace something.
tr	Transpose.
◯	Spell correctly.
¶	Indent paragraph.
/	Make a lowercase letter.

USING COMPUTERS

Using a computer, you can write and revise easily because it's simple to make changes. If you don't like where you put a sentence, you can move it without retyping it. Some computers also have a thesaurus or spell-check program.

Thesaurus

You can use a computerized **thesaurus** to replace overused words with more specific ones. Highlight each overused word. Then have the thesaurus search for another word to replace it.

Spell-Check

Use a **spell-check** program to help you check your spelling. It will show you many misspelled words. However, some spelling errors only you can find. These are words that are spelled correctly but are used incorrectly.

Chris filled out his camp <u>from</u>.

From *is a correctly spelled word, so the spell-check cannot find it. The writer has misspelled* form.

When you proofread, use your computer to help you.

PROOFREADING STRATEGIES

A REVISED AND PROOFREAD DRAFT

Look at the changes one writer made to this first draft. The revisions are shown in blue ink. The proofreading changes are shown in red.

¶Juan stretched out his arms. Juan *and* took a deep breath. Mo was happy. *His dog,* Mo was jumpy. Mo was *and* playful. It was a sunny day. *but* The air was cool. Juan himself *was as* is excited. *as a puppy* His uncle had called yesterday and asked, "Could I talk you into a day of fishing?" now they were out in the middle of the lake where the sun was *a* bright. *spotlight in the sky* The water looked so good that Mo *tried* made an attempt to jump out of the boat they were in John looked across the lake at another boat. The *fisher* person had caught a *whopper!* fish.

Why do you think the writer moved this sentence?

What is better about the changes made to the last sentence?

How are the proofreading changes different from the other changes?

THE FINAL DRAFT

The final draft should be read one last time for errors that may have been missed during proofreading.

Juan stretched out his arms and took a deep breath. It was a sunny day, but the air was cool. His dog, Mo, was happy, jumpy, and playful. Juan himself was as excited as a puppy. His uncle had called yesterday and asked, "Could I talk you into a day of fishing?" Now they were out in the middle of the lake, where the sun was a bright spotlight in the sky. The water looked so good that Mo tried to jump out of the boat. Juan looked across the lake at another boat. The fisher had caught a whopper!

The writing is neat and easy to read.

Space is left at the top and sides. Why is it a good idea to leave this space?

Publishing Your Writing

Publishing means sharing your work with others. How you share your work will depend on your task, audience, and purpose. There are many ways to do this. Here are some ideas.

- **Write and share a final draft on paper.**
- **Send a disk with your writing on it to a friend who can read it at a computer terminal.**
- **Create a video presentation by reading your work in front of a video camera.**
- **Make a cover and a title page for your writing and turn it into a book.**
- **Make a tape recording to listen to.**
- **Create a graphic display of your writing.**

Remember your TAP when you choose how to publish.

Here are some more ways you can share your writing with others:

- **Mail or fax your writing to the person you want to read it.**

- **Turn a story into a play and perform it.**

- **Send your writing to a publisher.**

- **Illustrate a story and turn it into a picture book.**

- **Stage a debate using persuasive writing.**

- **Create graphics for a research report and present the report orally.**

- **Gather stories and poems written by all your classmates, and make a table of contents to create a class book.**

- **Combine news stories and create headlines to make a class newspaper.**

- **Add sound effects and background music to give a dramatic reading.**

- **Have volunteer performers dance to or act out your poem or story as you read it aloud.**

What other ways can you think of to share your writing?

Use your imagination to create even more ways to share your writing.

Writing Approaches

You write every day in different ways. You write for school assignments, but you also write when you jot down a message or make a list of things to do. Sometimes you write alone. Other times you write in a group. There are many different ways to write, but all help you sort ideas and think through problems.

Writing in a group requires teamwork!

WRITING IN A GROUP

One of the best ways to discover ideas is to work as a member of a group. Here are some suggested roles.

- The **Reader** reads aloud questions, directions, and other information.

- The **Questioner** raises questions.

- The **Recorder** takes notes, records answers, and writes the final draft.

- The **Checker** proofreads.

SHARED WRITING

In shared writing, another person helps you think of ideas for writing and discusses your ideas with you. The other person does all the writing. Usually, the other person is a teacher or family member. Shared writing is useful because it helps you think through your ideas.

In shared writing, someone else records your ideas.

WRITING TO LEARN

Writing to learn is any writing that you use as a tool to help you learn. It can be short, unplanned, and even unedited. You are writing to learn whenever you

- **make notes to compare two things.**
- **summarize in a sentence or two.**
- **write an observation.**
- **classify, or put ideas into groups.**
- **make a judgment.**
- **tell what something means to you.**

Writing to Learn Every Day

Use writing to learn as a tool for thinking in these ways:

- **At the end of a discussion, jot down your thoughts. Think about what someone has said or review what you have heard.**

- **At the beginning of an assignment, write questions you want answered. Doing this will help focus your thoughts.**

- **Before you start a project, write out a plan.**

Learning Log

You can use writing as a tool for thinking by taking notes in a **learning log**. Divide sheets of paper into two columns. In the left column, write notes. In the right column, write thoughts or questions.

The California Gold Rush	
1848—gold found in California	This will probably be big business.
Two million settlers move west.	Are there enough resources for them?

Writing Forms

Writing to Entertain or Express

Performers may act, sing, or dance to entertain an audience and to express themselves. An author has a similar purpose when writing to **entertain** readers and to **express** feelings and ideas. If you like to tell stories, read poetry, or act, you can put your ideas on paper. If you need some help in writing, ask yourself questions such as these.

A time line or story map can help you organize events.

PREWRITING

Choosing a Topic

- **What might make an interesting story, folktale, poem, or play?**

- **Will my characters be real or imaginary?**

- **How might I use sensory details?**

Gathering and Organizing Details

- **What is my setting?**

- **Who are my characters?**

- **What problem will the characters have?**

- **Will a story map help me?**

DRAFTING

- Am I following my story map?
- Does my story have a beginning, a middle, and an ending?
- Do my characters solve their problem?

RESPONDING AND REVISING

- Have I used vivid details?
- Do I identify characters and a setting?
- Are events in the correct order?

PROOFREADING

- Have I used correct grammar and spelling?
- Is my dialogue punctuated correctly?

PUBLISHING

- Is my final copy neatly written or typed?
- What is the best way I can share my writing?

EXPRESSIVE WRITING MODELS

Perfect!

PURPOSES FOR WRITING

MODEL: STORY

In a **story,** a writer tells about one main idea. A story has characters, a plot, and a setting. The plot has a beginning, a middle, and an ending.

title

The Answering Machine
with Wings

**beginning
(with characters
and setting)**

Mom and I were painting when the phone rang. I ran to answer it. It was Dad.

I put the receiver down on the table by the bird cage and went to get Mom. That's when Polly, our parrot, took over.

"Hello," said Polly. "Hi, honey. Okay. I love you. Bye-bye."

**middle
(with
problem)**

Mom grabbed the phone, but it was too late. Dad had hung up. Now we didn't know when or where his plane would land. Only Polly knew what Dad had said.

I suggested we call the airport, but Mom said we didn't know a flight number.

Then Polly squawked. "Okay, honey. Three o'clock, Gate 24."

**ending
(with problem solved)**

Mom and I laughed. Soon we had a new answering machine — one with wings!

MODEL: FOLKTALE

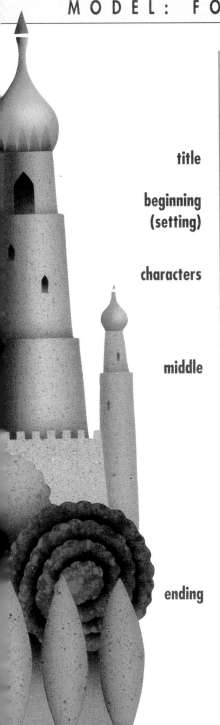

*A **folktale** is a special story that was first told orally and has been passed from one storyteller to another. In many folktales, animals act like people.*

title

The Lonely King's Friend

beginning
(setting)

Once there was a lonely king in India who kept canaries as pets. He loved to listen to their songs, but he was still lonely.

characters

One day the king's guards found a parrot and gave it to the king. When the canaries sang, the parrot screeched. The king put his hands over his ears.

middle

"Oh, how can this be?" the king said loudly. "I want you to take away this awful bird!"

"Oh, how can this be?" answered the parrot loudly.

Now the king realized he had something special. He told his guards to leave the unusual bird.

"I haven't had a friend to talk to in a while," said the king.

"Oh, how can this be?" answered the bird.

ending

"Well, let me tell you," said the king. The two of them talked for hours—and parrots have talked ever since.

MODEL: RHYMED POEM

A **poem** paints a picture or expresses a feeling with words. It may repeat words or letter sounds. It may have **rhyme**. It often has a definite **rhythm**, or beat.

title

words that rhyme (underlined)

The Parrot

Perched on the cage swing,
Swaying to and <u>fro</u>,
"Polly want a cracker,"
She wanted me to <u>know</u>.

Perched on my shoulder,
Cocking her <u>head</u>,
"Polly want a cracker,"
The parrot <u>said</u>.

Perched on my shoulder,
Looking at my <u>hand</u>,
"Polly want a cracker,"
Was her <u>demand</u>.

Perched on my finger,
Working her <u>beak</u>,
Now Polly has a cracker
And she can't <u>speak</u>.

MODEL: UNRHYMED POEM

A **poem** doesn't have to have rhyme. It can paint a word picture using colorful words and comparisons. Read the poem on page 40. Then see how the same poem can be written without rhyme.

title

word that compares (underlined)

The Parrot

<u>Like</u> a child on a park swing,
it sways to and fro.

<u>Like</u> a pup wanting a bone,
it begs for a cracker.

<u>Like</u> a mosquito buzzing,
it constantly bothers.

<u>Like</u> a babe with a bottle,
it is finally silent.

MODEL: PLAY

A **play** is a story meant to be acted out. It has characters, one or more settings, and a plot. Conversation in a play is called **dialogue**. The play's **stage directions** tell the characters how to move, act, and speak. This model shows how the story on page 38 could be written as a play.

title

The Answering Machine with Wings

beginning

NARRATOR: This is the Mackeen family den. That's Polly, the parrot, in the bird cage by the telephone. Mrs. Mackeen and her daughter Sara are painting in another room when the telephone rings.

stage directions in parentheses

SARA (running to pick up the phone): Hello. Hi, Daddy. Mom's painting. I'll go get her.

MRS. MACKEEN (calling loudly): Who is it?

SARA (shouting): It's Dad!

dialogue

MRS. MACKEEN (still shouting): Come wash this paintbrush so I can talk to him!

SARA (placing phone down by the bird cage and exiting): Okay, Mom.

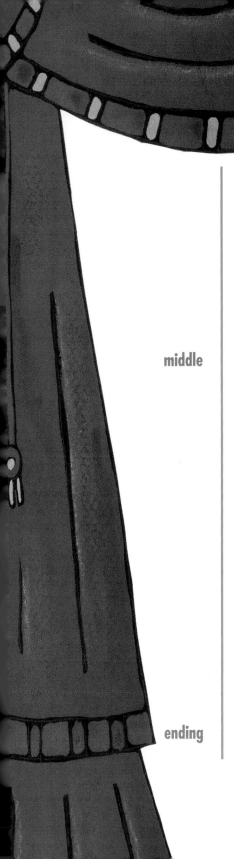

POLLY (bending down to phone): Hello. Hi, Honey. Okay. I love you. Bye-bye.

MRS. MACKEEN (racing into room and grabbing phone): Hello. Hello! (pause) Oh, no!

SARA (entering room): What's the matter?

middle

MRS. MACKEEN (shocked): He hung up. Now I don't know which gate to meet him at. I don't even know when his plane lands.

SARA: Can't we call the airport?

POLLY (squawking): That's right. Airport.

MRS. MACKEEN (shaking her head): No. I don't have a flight number. Now only Polly knows what he said.

POLLY (swinging on her swing): Okay, Honey. Three o'clock. Gate 24.

MRS. MACKEEN (laughing): How do you like that? We have a new answering machine.

ending

SARA (also laughing): An answering machine with wings! Good girl, Polly.

Writing to Describe

Have you ever written about a person you met, a place you visited, or a sporting event you saw? If you have, your purpose was to **describe** a specific person, place, or thing to an audience. In a description, the details you use help your audience see, feel, hear, and maybe even taste and smell what you describe. Think about these questions when your purpose for writing is to describe.

Descriptive writing uses sensory details.

PREWRITING

Choosing a Topic

- Will I write about a person, a place, a thing, or an event?

- Do I know the topic well?

- Will the topic interest my audience?

Gathering and Organizing Details

- What details will I use?

- Will my details appeal to the senses?

D R A F T I N G

- **What will my topic sentence be?**

- **Do my details all help describe my topic?**

R E S P O N D I N G
A N D   R E V I S I N G

- **Does my topic sentence tell what I am describing?**

- **Do my sentences appeal to the senses?**

- **Are there details I can add?**

P R O O F R E A D I N G

- **Have I spelled everything correctly?**

- **Have I used capitalization and punctuation correctly?**

P U B L I S H I N G

- **How will I title my description?**

- **How can I share my description with others?**

- **Will pictures or diagrams make the description clearer?**

DESCRIPTIVE WRITING MODELS

MODEL: DESCRIPTIVE PARAGRAPH

A **descriptive paragraph** creates a word picture. It describes a person, a place, an object, or an event. It includes details that let the reader see, feel, hear, and sometimes taste and smell what is being described.

title

Morning Practice

topic sentence

colorful words that appeal to the senses in detail sentences

The skater appeared out of the morning mist. Her strong body swayed from side to side. Her arms, legs, and long brown ponytail were swinging in time to the whoosh, whoosh of her skates on the hard road. As she came nearer, the still air stirred, bringing the aroma of breakfast muffins. Then, like a gust of wind, she passed by. I turned to watch as she vanished into the gray dawn.

MODEL: DESCRIPTIVE ESSAY

*A **descriptive essay** creates a word picture as it tells about one subject. It has a beginning, middle, and ending. Like a descriptive paragraph, it includes sensory details.*

beginning that tells what you will describe

supporting paragraphs with sensory details

The Contest

My older brothers and I have won several roller-skating contests. We practice for hours every weekend in Emerson Park. Last weekend, we were in our most unusual contest of all when we raced against nature.

When we walked into the park, the sun was bright and warm. My brothers and I laced up our skates and started down the narrow path. We skated in and out of patches of light and dark as we sped past huge oak trees. We stopped only once, to buy cool, refreshing cherry ice pops.

Halfway through the park and the ice pops, we felt a sudden chill. Gray clouds blocked the sun. Suddenly, the park was like a dark tunnel. The wind tossed twigs and acorns at our legs. Thunder rumbled so loudly that it shook the ground. Beads of sweat dotted our foreheads as we skated faster, racing the oncoming storm. Our leg muscles burned. Our hearts pounded. At last, we saw the park exit.

ending

We had won our race with the storm. We reached home just as the rain began. A flash of lightning reminded me of a camera flash going off to record our biggest race of all.

DESCRIPTIVE WRITING

MODEL: CHARACTER SKETCH

*In a **character sketch**, a writer describes a real or an imaginary person.*

topic sentence

Amy Johnson in The New Skates is the youngest member of the Sport Barn's skating team. At four feet, two inches, she is a petite nine-year-old. But what Amy lacks in size, she makes up in strength.

how character looks and acts

Amy began skating at the age of six. To keep up with her older brothers, she practices every day. Amy likes to skate for exercise and for fun. She began practicing small turns in her basement when she couldn't skate outdoors.

what makes the character special

When Amy first applied for a spot on the team, the store owners thought she was too young. But Amy's skill, courage, and willingness not to give up soon changed the owners' minds. Amy is now the team's most valuable member.

Writing to Inform

What would you like to know more about? What information might you share with your readers that is new and interesting? When you write to share facts and observations about a topic, you are writing to **inform**. Here are some things to think about when your purpose for writing is to inform.

PREWRITING

Choosing a Topic

- Will I write about something I know, or will I research a topic?

- What topic would other people find interesting?

- Where will I find information on this topic?

Gathering Information

- What details and facts do I need to include?

- What, if any, outside resources will I need to find those facts?

HOW TO MAKE
BREAKFAST

DRAFTING

- Am I including background knowledge my audience needs?

- Am I using any notes I made on note cards?

RESPONDING AND REVISING

- Have I presented the information clearly and in the right order?

- Are there any facts that I should add?

- Is there any information that doesn't really belong?

PROOFREADING

- Did I spell all proper nouns and technical terms correctly?

- Did I capitalize all proper nouns?

PUBLISHING

- What is the best way to share my information with others?

- Are there any photographs or illustrations that would make the information clearer?

INFORMATIVE WRITING MODELS

MODEL: PERSONAL NARRATIVE

*In a **personal narrative**, a writer tells about an experience in his or her life.*

strong beginning

I never thought a homework assignment would make me famous at school, but it did. It began when my teacher, Mr. Reyes, asked us to write about a way we could help save the earth.

middle that describes events in time order

Once I had an idea about paper recycling, I wrote quickly. I shared my idea first with my class. Then I shared it with the whole school during assembly. Before I knew it, the Baxter plan was in use.

Each class now has boxes for white and colored paper. If only one side of a piece of paper has been used, it goes into a box. Other students then use the blank side for writing rough drafts, taking notes, or drawing and other art projects.

ending

I'm proud to know I made a difference. I'm even prouder that my classmates helped me make that difference. You'd be amazed at how much paper we save!

MODEL: PARAGRAPH OF INFORMATION

A **paragraph of information** gives facts about one topic.

title

Where Does All the Paper Go?

topic sentence

When paper is recycled, it doesn't just become recycled paper. It is made into many different new products. Some of

facts

these products include boxes for cereal and shoes. Recycled paper can also be used to make egg cartons, paper towels, and tissues. Some recycled paper helps people send messages to friends and family when it becomes greeting cards. Along with other resources, paper waste becomes plaster board for the walls of homes and tar paper for under roofs. Even our cars may have paper waste in the form of stiffening for doors and sun visors.

EXPOSITORY WRITING

MODEL:
HOW-TO PARAGRAPH

*A **how-to paragraph** gives directions or explains how to do something. Steps are given in time order.*

How to Recycle Paper at Home

topic sentence

materials needed

time-order words in steps

Help save trees by recycling paper at home. First, gather all your old and unwanted newspapers, magazines, and catalogs. Then separate the newspapers from glossy paper inserts. The inserts go with magazines and catalogs to be recycled. Next, place each kind of paper in a separate pile. When you have a bundle that is about 10 inches high, tie it up both lengthwise and around the middle with strong string. Finally, store your paper bundles in a dry place until recycling pickup day. If your community doesn't have a pickup, find out where you can take your paper to be recycled.

MODEL:
HOW-TO ESSAY

*A **how-to essay** explains in several paragraphs how to do something. It has a beginning, a middle, and an ending. It gives steps in time order.*

Homemade Recycled Paper

topic sentence that tells
what is being explained

Making your own recycled paper with an adult family member can be fun and will help save trees. You will need two newspaper pages, a large pan that is 3 inches deep, two pieces of window screen cut to fit the pan, a blender, and some water.

materials needed

explanatory
paragraphs in
time order

First, tear the newspaper into tiny pieces. Ask a family member to put the pieces in a blender, add 4 cups of water, place the lid on the blender, and turn it on. The thick mixture that forms is called <u>pulp</u>.

Next, put an inch of water in the pan. Place one screen in the pan and pour in the pulp. Then carefully lift the screen and shake it gently from side to side to even out the pulp and let the water drain.

ending

Finally, place the second screen over the pulp, and squeeze to remove excess water. Set the screens and pulp aside to dry into your very own recycled paper.

MODEL: PARAGRAPH THAT COMPARES

In a **paragraph that compares**, a writer shows how two people, places, or things are alike.

topic sentence

at least three likenesses

The basic processes for making recycled and unrecycled paper are alike in some ways. Both involve cooking material to make a pulp. Also, in both cases the pulp must be strained to remove impurities. Both kinds of paper are formed into sheets by a kind of press.

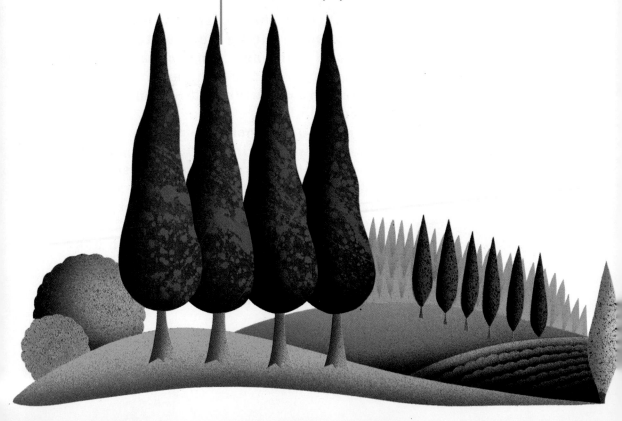

MODEL: PARAGRAPH THAT CONTRASTS

In a **paragraph that contrasts**, a writer shows how two people, places, or things are different.

topic sentence

differences

The processes for making regular paper and recycled paper are different in a couple of ways. The traditional process for making paper begins with wood. Liquid chemicals must be added to turn the wood into a pulp. The process for making recycled paper begins with waste paper. Water is added to moisten and soften the paper. Water and chemicals wash away old inks. No such washing is needed with unrecycled paper.

EXPOSITORY WRITING

MODEL: WRITING FOR MATH

*When you write a story problem or express a math equation in words, you are **writing for math.** When you write a story problem, always include enough information for solving the problem.*

Recycled paper is made into grocery bags. The bags come in packages of 75. How many bags are in 40 packages?

Use the Problem-Solving Think Along™ below to help you use writing to solve problems.

Understand

1. Retell the problem in your own words.

2. Restate the question as a fill-in-the-blank sentence.

3. List the information given.

Plan

4. List problem-solving strategies you can use.

5. Predict what your answer will be.

Solve

6. Show how you solved the problem.

7. Write your answer in a complete sentence.

Look Back

8. Tell how you know your answer is reasonable.

9. Describe another way you could have solved the problem.

*When you write observations from an experiment, you are **writing for science**. Include a title, purpose, materials, procedure, observations, and conclusions.*

What Decomposes in Moist Soil?

Purpose: To find out which materials break down in moist soil

Materials: 2 apple cores, 2 shoe boxes, 2 glass bottles, 2 pieces of plastic

Procedure:

1. Bury one of each of the materials in moist soil. Bury the remaining materials in dry soil.

2. Dig up the materials in one month.

Observations: In the moist soil, the apple core had disappeared and the shoe box was falling apart. The bottle and the piece of plastic were unchanged. In the dry soil, the apple core had partly disappeared and the shoe box was limp. The bottle and plastic were unchanged.

Conclusions: In moist soil, the apple core decomposed and the shoe box soon would. The glass and plastic would not. Moist soil speeds up the decomposition of some materials.

NEWS INTERVIEW

In a **news story**, *a reporter presents information to an audience. Often a reporter conducts an interview in which he or she asks questions to get information for the news story.*

Interviewing Techniques

Here are some things to think about when conducting an interview:

- **What do I already know about this person? What can I find out ahead of time?**

- **What questions can I ask to find out** *who, what, when, where, why,* **and** *how?*

- **Have I avoided questions with yes or no answers?**

Sample Interview Questions

Who?	1. What is your full name? (Check spelling.)
What?	2. What is your project?
When?	3. When did you start your project?
Where?	4. Where did you do the project?
Why?	5. Why did you decide to do this project?
How?	6. How did you complete your project?

MODEL: NEWS STORY

A **news story** *tells* who, what, when, where, *and sometimes* why *and* how. *It begins with a* **headline** *containing a strong verb.*

headline

paragraph telling *who, what, when, and where*

additional details about the event

Local Boy Saves the Earth

On April 10, Sean Baxter, a student at Lincoln School in Amherst, turned a homework assignment into a school project to save the earth.

When Sean was told by his fourth-grade teacher, Mr. Hugo Reyes, to write about a way students could save the earth, he didn't know what to write.

"I started several times," says Sean, "and threw each piece of paper away. When I ran out of paper, I wrote on the backs of papers in the trash. That's when I got my idea."

Sean's idea was to place boxes for white and colored paper in each classroom. If only one side of a piece is used, it is put into a box for reuse.

Sean shared his idea in assembly on April 10. The "Baxter Plan" was adopted that day.

EXPOSITORY/NARRATIVE WRITING

MODEL: RESEARCH REPORT OUTLINE

To write a **research report,** *a writer gathers facts from different sources, takes notes, and makes an* **outline.** *The notes and outline are used to write about the topic. The sources are usually listed at the end of the report.*

Outline

Outlines follow a certain form. Main ideas are shown with Roman numerals. Subtopics are shown with capital letters.

From Used Paper to New

   I. Introduction
  II. How paper is recycled
      A. Passing inspection
      B. Forming the pulp
      C. Changing the pulp into paper
 III. Conclusion

*A **research report** provides information about a topic. This short report follows the outline on page 62. Reports can be several pages long.*

title

introduction that
identifies topic

body with information
on subtopics

conclusion

From Used Paper to New

In 1800, English inventor Matthias Koops found a way to make new paper from old paper. In the early 1900s, some paper mills in the United States began using his idea, but it took almost another hundred years for paper recycling to become popular.

Most paper mills now use his basic steps. First, the old paper is inspected for unwanted objects. Then it is cooked with hot water in a machine called a hydrapulper, which forms a pulp. The pulp goes through several washers and spinners to remove inks, dyes, and small objects. Next, it is fed onto wire mesh, where rollers press out the water. Heated rollers then iron the pulp smooth.

Although the idea of recycling paper is not new, people are just realizing its value now. Recycling paper offers an added bonus. It costs a lot less than making new paper.

63

Writing to Persuade

Have you ever tried to convince someone to let you do something or to agree with your opinion? If you have, your purpose was to **persuade**. Persuasion is one of the most useful forms of writing because it can make people take action. Ask yourself these questions if you need help writing to persuade.

Saving your strongest fact for last has a powerful effect on readers.

PREWRITING

Choosing a Topic

- **What topic do I feel strongly about?**

- **Will this topic interest my audience?**

Gathering and Organizing Details

- **What facts can I use to support my opinion?**

- **Which is the most important fact?**

DRAFTING

- Have I stated my opinion clearly?
- Did I put my strongest fact last?

RESPONDING AND REVISING

- Do I need to make my opinion or facts clearer?
- Will my audience be convinced?

PROOFREADING

- Have I checked my grammar, spelling, and punctuation?
- Are my paragraphs indented?

PUBLISHING

- What would be the best way to present my work?
- Will visuals help me convince my audience?

PERSUASIVE WRITING MODELS

MODEL: PERSUASIVE PARAGRAPH

In a **persuasive paragraph,** a writer tells his or her opinion about a topic. The writer tries to convince the audience to agree with that opinion and to take action.

opinion

reasons/facts

restated opinion/ request for action

I am strongly in favor of having small pets like rabbits at school. Animals are fun and educational to watch. Many kinds of pets are intelligent and can be trained to do things. Also, class members learn responsibility by having to take care of the pets' food and their homes. There are many small pets at the Nature Society that need good homes because they have been hurt or are unwanted. I think every class in this school should have a class pet!

MODEL: PERSUASIVE ESSAY

*A **persuasive essay** has a beginning, a middle with paragraphs supporting the writer's opinion, and an ending.*

title

Pets Are an Education

beginning with opinion stated

A favorite topic in science this year has been animal life. It is fascinating to watch animals in their environment. Therefore, I strongly urge everyone to vote "yes" for getting a small pet for our classroom for three reasons.

middle with reasons to support opinion

First, an animal would be interesting to watch. Even a frog or a small rabbit could help us learn about animal behavior. We read about animals, but many of us have never seen a real frog or rabbit.

Also, we can provide a natural environment. We have a nature court in which a pet would feel at home and be safe.

strongest reason

A third reason is for the pets. Many hurt or unwanted animals are cared for at the Nature Society. They need good homes. They cannot survive in nature alone. We can show responsibility by adopting one of these animals.

ending with restated opinion or request for action

Think of yourselves and the animals. Vote "yes" for a class pet!

MODEL:
BOOK REVIEW

In a **book review,** a writer tells what a book is about without telling the whole story. The review also gives the writer's opinion of the book and suggests whether others should read it.

title

author

main characters

setting

summary of book

why it should be read

The Incredible Journey

The Incredible Journey by Sheila Burnford is an incredible book. It tells the story of a cat, Tao, and two dogs, Bodger and Luath, that set out across 250 miles of Canadian wilderness searching for their way home to the family they love.

When the adventure begins, the pets are staying with a friend while the family is away. Due to a mixup, the pets aren't missed for several weeks when they begin their journey. The pets are chased by wild animals, delayed by people, and challenged by nature.

You'll laugh and cry as you journey home with these three animals. They are courageous and true. This book is a must for animal lovers.

MODEL: TELEVISION OR MOVIE REVIEW

In a **television** or **movie review**, a writer tells about a program or movie, gives an opinion on it, and says whether others should watch it.

title

Homeward Bound

setting/main characters

Homeward Bound is a new movie based on Sheila Burnford's popular novel The Incredible Journey. It tells the story of a cat, Sassy, and two dogs, Chance and Shadow, that set out across the California wilderness to find their way home to the family they love.

summary

This film closely follows the novel, with one major exception. In the movie, the animals have voices and talk. Some viewers will like this difference, but it may bother others. In either

why it should be seen

case, this is not a movie to be missed. The scenery is beautiful and the message of loyalty and love is great.

PERSUASIVE/EXPOSITORY WRITING

SPEECH OR ORAL REPORT

In a **speech** or an **oral report,** the speaker shares information with his or her audience. Usually, the information given informs the listeners about some topic. It may also try to persuade them to do or not to do something.

Follow these tips when preparing a speech or an oral report.

- Use note cards or an outline when you give your report.

- When possible, use visuals such as charts, slides, or pictures to give information and to help keep your audience's attention.

When the time comes to give your speech or oral report, remember these tips:

- Speak clearly and loudly. Do not speak too slowly or too quickly.

- Look at your audience. Refer to your notes only when you need them. (To be able to do this, you should practice beforehand.)

- Afterwards, thank your audience. Ask if there are any questions.

PERSUASIVE/EXPOSITORY WRITING

"Dogs are more than just pets and should be treated as such. Many are real heroes. They work their whole lives at jobs such as herding sheep . . ."

"Balto was a famous Eskimo sled dog. In 1925, he led a dog team 650 miles through a blizzard to carry a desperately needed diphtheria serum . . ."

The following items show how a speaker might use notes to present an oral report.

I   *Introduction*
   a. more than pets—heroes
   B. sheep dogs, guide dogs, police dogs
   C. played important part in history

II. *Balto (Slide 1)*
   a. Eskimo sled dog
   B. in 1925 went 650 miles in blizzard
   C. carried diphtheria serum from Nenana to Nome

III. *Laika (Slide 2)*
   a. first space traveler
   B. November 3, 1957—Soviet satellite Sputnik II
   C. paved way for humans in space

IV. *Conclusion*
   a. dogs intelligent—trained for jobs
   B. do important things (some things humans can't)
   C. should be treated well

Everyday Writing

Have you ever thought about the kinds of writing you do every day, outside of school? Name some. Were some of these writing forms on your list?

friendly letter	**invitation**	**messages**
business letter	**journal or diary**	**notes**
thank-you note	**lists**	**summaries**

You don't often need the steps of the writing process for everyday writing. Sometimes, though, you may find it helpful to ask yourself these questions.

Most everyday writing is informal. Write freely!

PREWRITING

Choosing a Topic

- What are my task and my purpose?

- Who is my audience?

Gathering and Organizing Details

- What information should I include?

- Do I need to include dates, times, addresses, or telephone numbers?

D R A F T I N G

- Are events in the order I need them to be?

- Have I included all necessary parts?

R E S P O N D I N G
A N D   R E V I S I N G

- Have I accomplished my purpose?

- Are there details I want to add or cut?

P R O O F R E A D I N G

- Are names and addresses spelled correctly?

- Do I need to worry about errors in grammar or punctuation?

P U B L I S H I N G

- Do I need to publish this writing, or is it just for me?

- Will I handwrite my final copy?

- Do I need an envelope?

MODEL: JOURNAL

A **journal** is a place where you record events, ideas, and feelings. Each dated piece in the journal is called an **entry**.

February 18, 1995

date of entry

what happened

My second day in Florida began with a dip in the pool. Then Grandma took me to an aquarium near her home. That's where I saw my first manatee. It was huge! It was ten feet long and weighed 1,500 pounds. It looked like a walrus but without tusks. Grandma said the manatee, Arnold, had been hurt. He was rescued by the Florida Marine Patrol and brought to the aquarium to be cared for. The visit got me interested in manatees. Tomorrow, Grandma and I are going to adopt one!

why it is important

DESCRIPTIVE/NARRATIVE WRITING

A **dialogue journal** is a journal in which you exchange ideas and feelings with someone else. You might share a dialogue journal with a teacher, a friend, or a family member.

date

February 27, 1995

student's journal comment

The best thing about my Florida midwinter vacation was seeing a manatee. My grandma also adopted one for me. His name is Oscar. The Manatee Club gave me his picture and his life story.

signature

Carl

date

March 1, 1995

teacher's response

Carl,

Adopting a manatee sounds like a wonderful idea! Could you find out how the class might adopt one? I hope you'll share Oscar's picture with us.

signature

Mrs. Cassidy

DESCRIPTIVE/NARRATIVE WRITING

MODEL: FRIENDLY LETTER

In a **friendly letter**, a person writes to someone he or she knows. A friendly letter has a heading, a greeting, a body, a closing, and a signature. In the heading, include a comma between the city and state and between the day of the month and the year.

**heading
(writer's address
and date)**

> 11 West End Avenue
> Summit, NJ 07901
> March 1, 1995

greeting

Dear Chris,

> I wish you had come to Florida with me. Grandma and I had fun, but we really missed you.

body

> The best part of my trip was seeing a manatee at an aquarium. It looked like a walrus without tusks.
>
> Now I'm a manatee fan. Grandma adopted one for me! Keep checking your mail. She adopted one for you, too! Write and tell me about it.

**closing
signature**

> Your friend,
> Carl

DESCRIPTIVE/NARRATIVE WRITING

*A **business letter** can ask for or share information about business, order something, or praise or complain about a product or service. It uses formal language but has the same parts as a friendly letter, plus an **inside address**.*

heading

*11 West End Avenue
Summit, NJ 07901
March 4, 1995*

inside address

*Mr. Jack Shi
Manatee Club
23 Kaley Avenue
DeLand, FL 32720*

greeting

Dear Mr. Shi:

body

Please send me information about how my class can adopt a manatee. I learned of your club when I was in Florida.

My grandmother adopted a manatee for me. When I told my classmates, they wanted to find out more about these unusual animals and adopt one, too.

I hope to hear from you soon. Thank you.

**closing
signature**

*Sincerely,
Carl Leewood*

77

MODEL: ENVELOPE

*A letter is sent in an **envelope** that shows the receiver's address and return address. A postal abbreviation for each state and a ZIP code are included.*

return address

receiver's address

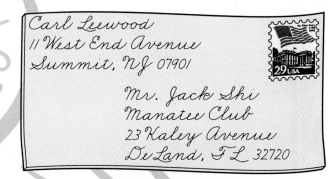

Carl Leewood
11 West End Avenue
Summit, NJ 07901

Mr. Jack Shi
Manatee Club
23 Kaley Avenue
DeLand, FL 32720

Postal Abbreviations

Alabama AL	Kentucky KY	Ohio OH
Alaska AK	Louisiana LA	Oklahoma OK
Arizona AZ	Maine ME	Oregon OR
Arkansas AR	Maryland MD	Pennsylvania PA
California CA	Massachusetts MA	Rhode Island RI
Colorado CO	Michigan MI	South Carolina SC
Connecticut CT	Minnesota MN	South Dakota SD
Delaware DE	Mississippi MS	Tennessee TN
District of	Missouri MO	Texas TX
Columbia DC	Montana MT	Utah UT
Florida FL	Nebraska NE	Vermont VT
Georgia GA	Nevada NV	Virginia VA
Hawaii HI	New Hampshire NH	Washington WA
Idaho ID	New Jersey NJ	West Virginia WV
Illinois IL	New Mexico NM	Wisconsin WI
Indiana IN	New York NY	Wyoming WY
Iowa IA	North Carolina NC	
Kansas KS	North Dakota ND	

*A **message** states information received in person or by telephone. It tells whom the message is for and what it is about. It also tells the date and time of the message and the name of the person taking the message. Ask the person leaving the message to spell or repeat anything that is unclear.*

day and time	Saturday 11:30 a.m.
name of person message is for	Carl,
name of caller	Mrs. Cassidy called. The
message	information on the class manatee, Sebastian, has arrived. Call her
telephone number of caller	at the school at 555-4215 before 1 p.m. if you want to see it.
recorder's name	Pat

F O R M

*A **form** is a sheet of paper with blanks used to write in information. Some of the reasons you fill out forms are to apply for a job, enter a contest, order from a catalog, or join a club.*

Here are some tips for filling out forms.

- Read the whole form before you begin to write.

- Be alert for directions that tell you to use pencil or pen.

- Check carefully to see where you should write. The line on which your name should appear, for example, may not be right next to the word *Name*. Instead, it may be below or above it.

- Watch for directions that tell you to print instead of write. Always print or write neatly.

- Give all the information you are asked for. When you are finished, look over the form to be sure you have completed it correctly.

- Turn the form over to see if there are questions on both sides.

This is a form for a club. Note the directions at the beginning of the form.

Save the Manatee Club

Please print in ink.

Name ___Leewood_____Carl_____
          (last)   (first)

Address ___11 West End Avenue_____
            (Number and Street)

___Summit_____NJ_____07901____
   (City)   (State)   (ZIP)

Tel.# _(212) 555-2801_____ Age ___9____

Grade ___4_____ Teacher __Mrs. Cassidy__

School Name __Harris Elementary_____

Address __401 McLeod Avenue_____
           (Number and Street)

___Summit_____NJ_____07901____
   (City)   (State)   (ZIP)

Where did you learn about our club?
__an aquarium in Florida_____

I want information about a manatee for:
_____ myself _____X____ my class

MODELS: NOTES AND QUESTIONNAIRE

Notes *are a written record that help you remember information. You take notes in class to help you remember what you hear or read. You also take notes to write a research report or to study for a test.*

One of the best ways to take notes for a report or test is to use index cards. Use one card for each main idea. Add facts to the card.

topic

main idea as question

facts in your own words

source (book, author, page number)

> *Manatee Dangers*
>
> *How do people endanger manatees?*
> * *manatees hurt by boat propellers*
> * *pollution destroys feeding areas*
> *Endangered Wildlife* *by Adam Kroll, p. 98*

A **questionnaire** *is a written list of questions used to get information. The results can be used in reports and speeches.*

> **Grade 4 Survey on Manatees**
>
> **Harris Elementary School**
> 1. **Are you interested in adopting a manatee for your class?**
>
>   yes ____   no ____   maybe ____

MODEL: SUMMARY

*A **summary** is a brief statement of main points in the writer's own words. It contains only a main idea and a few related details. A summary helps the writer remember main points from source material such as films, observations, and printed materials.*

source

Manatees are large mammals also known as sea cows. They live only in water and can be found in the southeastern United States, South America, and Africa. They eat mostly water plants and can digest more than 100 pounds of plants each day. In some places in South America, they are used to keep waterways clean.

summary

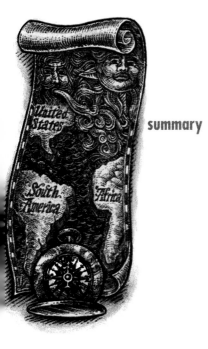

A manatee is a large water mammal that lives in the southeastern United States, South America, and Africa. It can digest over 100 pounds of plants a day and may be used to keep waterways clean.

Writing for a Test

Some kinds of test questions ask for a written response. They check whether you can organize thoughts, support ideas, write to a specific task and purpose, and use correct grammar. Remember these things when writing for a test.

Remember your TAP when writing for a test.

BEFORE THE TEST

- Listen carefully to the instructions your teacher or test-giver provides.

- Read the directions carefully.

- Ask any questions you have. (Some tests don't allow talking once testing starts.)

TIMED WRITING EXAMPLES

Written Prompt, page 87

Picture Prompt, page 88

DURING THE TEST

- Just as you begin, take time to identify your task, audience, and purpose.

- Work quietly without disturbing those around you.

AFTER THE TEST

- If you finish before time is up, go back and read what you have written. Make final corrections.

- Follow directions given at the beginning for what to do at the end. You may have to sit quietly while others finish.

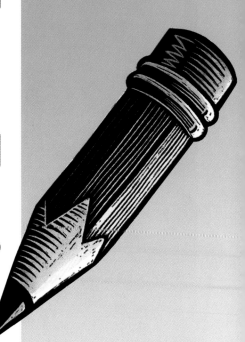

TIMED WRITING

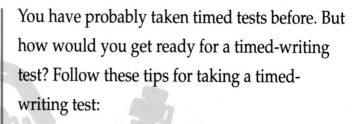

You have probably taken timed tests before. But how would you get ready for a timed-writing test? Follow these tips for taking a timed-writing test:

- **Stay calm.**

- **Plan ahead how much of the total time you will need to spend prewriting, drafting, revising, proofreading, and writing a final draft.**

- **Remember to check your task, audience, and purpose.**

- **Use your time wisely once you start writing.**

- **If you begin to run out of time while you are taking the test, decide whether to combine steps to finish on time.**

WRITTEN PROMPT

A **written prompt** is a statement or question that asks you to complete a writing task. Here is an example of a written prompt that asks the reader to tell a story about a personal experience.

Almost everyone has had an interesting experience visiting a new place.

Think about your own experience in a new place. It may have happened during a visit to another state, to a museum, or to some other place.

Now tell or recount a story to your reader about what happened when you visited this place.

NARRATIVE WRITING

These prompts ask the writer to "tell a story."

PERSUASIVE WRITING

These prompts ask the writer to "convince" or "persuade."

EXPOSITORY WRITING

These prompts ask the writer to "tell or explain why."

DESCRIPTIVE WRITING

These prompts ask the writer to "describe" something.

PICTURE PROMPT

A **picture prompt** is a statement or question about a picture. It asks the writer to tell something about the picture. Here is an example of a picture prompt that asks the writer to use description.

Picture yourself in this scene. Write a composition for your teacher in which you tell what you see.

Grammar, Usage, and Mechanics

Grammar

Usage

Mechanics

SENTENCES

SENTENCE

A *sentence* is a group of words that expresses a complete thought. The words in a sentence should be in an order that makes sense. Begin every sentence with a capital letter, and end it with an end mark.

Circus acts are thousands of years old.

The ancient Romans probably held the first circuses.

These shows had several animal acts.

Riders balanced on horseback.

Lions were also part of the show.

A group of words that does not express a complete thought is not a sentence.

The first American circus in 1792.
   not a sentence

The first American circus was formed in 1792.
   sentence

Exercise 1

Read each group of words. Tell which are sentences.

1. The first American circus was formed in Philadelphia.
2. Early circuses were small shows.
3. Acrobats, clowns, and animals.
4. By 1870 America had ten large circuses.
5. These shows traveled from place to place.
6. The colorful circus wagons.
7. Children wanted to help.
8. Some children brought water for the elephants.
9. Others fed the horses.
10. And were glad to see the circus.

For additional practice, turn to pages 166–167.

Writing Application

Use complete sentences to describe an exciting performance you have seen.

SENTENCES

DECLARATIVE SENTENCE

A *declarative sentence* makes a statement. Use a period (.) at the end of a declarative sentence.

Everyone has some special talent.

Ricky draws great pictures.

Maria plays the guitar.

Henri is a fine storyteller.

I am a good listener.

INTERROGATIVE SENTENCE

An *interrogative sentence* asks a question. Use a question mark (?) at the end of an interrogative sentence.

What did Ricky draw today?

Will you teach me that song?

Did Henri finish his story?

How did the story end?

Can you tell that joke again?

Exercise 2

Read each sentence. Tell whether it is a statement or a question and what end punctuation to add.

1. Our class is planning a performance
2. How many people will attend
3. Maria will play three songs
4. Andy and Phuong will sing
5. Will they need a microphone
6. The theater is not a large space
7. Can Ricky paint the background
8. Should we stay and help him
9. We will celebrate after the show
10. Our parents will be proud of us

For additional practice, turn to pages 168–169.

EXCLAMATORY SENTENCE

An *exclamatory sentence* expresses strong feeling. Use an exclamation point (!) at the end of an exclamatory sentence.

The rabbit is about to escape!

We have to catch it!

Writing Application

Describe a special talent you have. Use a declarative, an interrogative, and an exclamatory sentence.

SENTENCES

IMPERATIVE SENTENCE

An *imperative sentence* gives a command. It often begins with an action word. Use a period (.) at the end of an imperative sentence.

Teach a friend something new.

Don't be afraid to try new things.

Exercise 3

Tell whether each sentence is declarative, interrogative, exclamatory, or imperative. Explain how you know.

1. What a good swimmer Mike is!
2. Did Felicia teach him how to swim?
3. A coach teaches easy things first.
4. Hold your breath underwater.
5. Kick your feet.
6. Mike learned quickly.
7. Can we watch him race?
8. He swam faster than all the others.

For additional practice, turn to pages 170–171.

Kids on Language

My name is Alex Loayza [aˈleks lō•īˈsə], and I was born in Peru, which is on the west side of South America. Most of the people of Peru speak Spanish.

When I was learning to write in English, I was surprised that the question mark and the exclamation point are used differently. In English, you have to get to the end of a sentence to find out whether it is a question or an exclamation. That's not so in Spanish.

For a question in Spanish, you put an upside-down question mark at the beginning of the sentence. Then you put a right-side-up question mark at the end. For an exclamation in Spanish, you put an upside-down exclamation point at the beginning of the sentence, and then you put a right-side-up exclamation point at the end.

Examples:

¿Qué hora es? (What time is it?)

¡Muchas gracias! (Many thanks!)

SENTENCES

SIMPLE SENTENCE

A sentence that expresses only one complete thought is a *simple sentence.*

Sylvia read about a writing contest.

She sent in a poem.

The poem is about friendship.

COMPOUND SENTENCE

A *compound sentence* is made up of two or more simple sentences joined by a word such as *and, or,* or *but.* These words are called **conjunctions**. Use a comma (,) before a conjunction that joins two sentences.

Judges read the poem, *and* they discussed it.

Three judges liked her poem, *but* two did not.

Several other poems were sent in, *but* none of the judges liked them.

The judges voted, *and* Sylvia's poem won.

They will call Sylvia, *or* they will write to her.

Exercise 4

Tell whether each sentence is a simple sentence or a compound sentence.

1. Our country is made up of "united" states, and they work together.

2. This was not always the case.

3. The Revolutionary War was won, but the new states were not concerned about each other.

4. Leaders wanted rules for a strong national government.

5. George Washington helped write the Constitution, and he was elected President.

6. He was popular, and many stories were heard about his deeds.

7. Did he really throw a coin across a river, or did people just think so?

8. George Washington was President for two terms.

For additional practice, turn to pages 172–173.

Writing Application

Use simple sentences and compound sentences to write a paragraph about your community.

SENTENCE PARTS

SUBJECT

Every sentence has two parts, a subject and a predicate. The *subject* of a sentence names the person or thing the sentence is about.

Most baseball players quit before age 40.

Satchel Paige played ball until age 59.

This famous pitcher was honored in 1971.

The National Baseball Hall of Fame made him a member.

PREDICATE

The *predicate* of a sentence tells what the person or thing is or does.

Some people *enjoy parachuting out of planes.*

Sylvia Brett *is the oldest female parachutist in the world.*

Ms. Brett *earned this title at the age of 80.*

Exercise 5

Identify the subject and the predicate in each sentence.

1. Ronald Reagan was the oldest person to become President.
2. This famous person was elected at age 69.
3. Some American Presidents lived for quite a long time.
4. John Adams was the second President of the United States.
5. Herbert Hoover was elected President in 1928.
6. Both men lived to the age of 90.
7. The oldest First Lady was 65 years old.
8. This woman was named Anna Harrison.
9. Anna Harrison married William Henry Harrison in 1795.
10. William Henry Harrison became President in 1840.

For additional practice, turn to pages 174–175.

Writing Application

Write about something you'd like to do when you are older. Then work with a partner to identify the subjects and predicates of your sentences.

SENTENCE PARTS

COMPLETE SUBJECT

The *complete subject* includes all the words that tell whom or what the sentence is about.

Agricultural fairs are the most common type of fair.

Most of these fairs also have contests for homemade foods.

Many groups of young people and adults try their luck.

SIMPLE SUBJECT

The *simple subject* is the main word or words in the complete subject of a sentence.

Many farm <u>children</u> raise pigs for fun.

These proud <u>owners</u> love their unusual pets.

The future <u>farmers</u> often enter their pigs in contests.

GRAMMAR

Exercise 6

Find the complete subject in each sentence. Then identify the simple subject.

1. The county's fair was the best ever this year.
2. My whole family went together.
3. The games on the midway had good prizes.
4. My little brother entered a ring-toss contest.
5. The lucky winner got a giant teddy bear.
6. Three big tents held the foods and the animals.
7. The finest chicken won a blue ribbon.
8. A plump hog won the livestock contest.
9. Many delicious foods made my mouth water.
10. The best preserves were made by my mother.

For additional practice, turn to pages 176–177.

Writing Application

Write some sentences about a contest held at a fair. Identify the complete and simple subjects in your sentences.

SENTENCE PARTS

COMPOUND SUBJECT

A *compound subject* is two or more subjects joined by *and* or *or*. These subjects share the same predicate.

A *child or an adult* can ride a bicycle.

Health *and* fitness are concerns of many bike riders.

Exercise 7

Tell the subjects each sentence has. Then point out the word that joins the parts of each compound subject.

1. Bicycle racing or cycling is the name of a popular sport.
2. Light frames and narrow tires are found on road-race bikes.
3. Individuals and teams can compete in races.
4. A short sprint or a long race may be timed.
5. Indoor tracks and outdoor courses are used.

For additional practice, turn to pages 178–179.

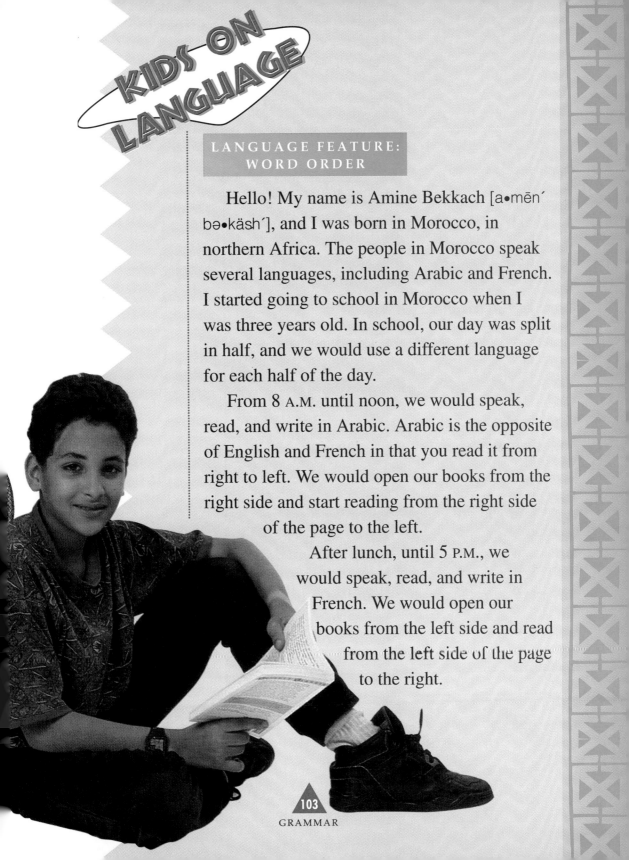

LANGUAGE FEATURE: WORD ORDER

Hello! My name is Amine Bekkach [a•mēn´ bə•käsh´], and I was born in Morocco, in northern Africa. The people in Morocco speak several languages, including Arabic and French. I started going to school in Morocco when I was three years old. In school, our day was split in half, and we would use a different language for each half of the day.

From 8 A.M. until noon, we would speak, read, and write in Arabic. Arabic is the opposite of English and French in that you read it from right to left. We would open our books from the right side and start reading from the right side of the page to the left.

After lunch, until 5 P.M., we would speak, read, and write in French. We would open our books from the left side and read from the left side of the page to the right.

103
GRAMMAR

SENTENCE PARTS

COMPLETE PREDICATE

The *complete predicate* includes all the words that tell what the subject of the sentence is or does.

Dogs *have a powerful sense of smell.*

These animals *are often used in rescue operations.*

Rescue dogs *follow the scent of the lost person.*

SIMPLE PREDICATE

The *simple predicate* is the main word or words in the complete predicate of a sentence.

A rescue dog _wears_ bells on its collar.

The trainer _may attach_ lights to a special vest on the dog.

The lost person _hears_ the dog's bells.

The person _sees_ the glistening lights, too.

GRAMMAR

Exercise 8

Find the complete predicate in each sentence.
Then identify the simple predicate.

1. Trainers coach rescue dogs for weeks.
2. The dogs have many valuable skills.
3. They practice in rain or snow.
4. The trainers work hard, too.
5. They run behind the dogs during a search.
6. Dogs and trainers often go nonstop for several hours.
7. Some rescue dogs work in avalanche country.
8. An avalanche may bury skiers under several feet of snow.
9. The dogs find the scent.
10. They dig quickly toward the skiers.

For additional practice, turn to pages 180–181.

For additional practice, turn to pages 180–181.

Writing Application

Write a story about an animal that helps people. Identify the simple predicate and the complete predicate in each sentence.

COMPOUND PREDICATE

A *compound predicate* is two or more predicates that have the same subject. The simple predicates in a compound predicate are usually joined by *and* or *or*.

Bears *chase or injure* sheep sometimes.

Guards *watch and protect* the flocks.

Exercise 9

Tell what the compound predicate is in each sentence.

1. Ranchers buy donkeys and make them guards.
2. A donkey lives and moves with the flock.
3. It sees intruders and springs to action.
4. It bares its teeth or brays.
5. The intruders usually turn and run away.

For additional practice, turn to pages 182–183.

NOUNS

NOUN

A *noun* is a word that names a person, a place, a thing, or an idea. A noun can tell who, what, or where.

farmer	den	forest	anger
people	barn	rabbit	power

Exercise 10

Read each sentence. Find the nouns.

1. The dog, fox, and wolf are related.
2. These animals are called canines.
3. The wolf is the largest member of the group.
4. This wild animal makes its home far from humans.
5. Those mammals have great endurance.
6. These athletes can run for miles.

For additional practice,
turn to pages 184–185.

Writing Application

Use nouns to tell about a wild animal you know something about.

GRAMMAR

NOUNS

COMMON NOUN

A *common noun* names any person, place, or thing. A common noun begins with a lowercase letter.

A *fox* has an orange *color* and a bushy *tail.*

Most *foxes* weigh eight to eleven *pounds.*

The *animals* do not form *packs.*

PROPER NOUN

A *proper noun* names a particular person, place, or thing. Begin each important word in a proper noun with a capital letter.

Foxes live on every continent but *Australia* and *Antarctica.*

Red foxes, kit foxes, and gray foxes live in *North America.*

In 1993, a boy found some of these animals near *San Diego, California.*

Ricky Johnston called the *San Diego Zoo.*

Exercise 11

Identify the common nouns and the proper nouns in these sentences.

1. Nan Lee is an authority on foxes.
2. This woman has studied the animals throughout the United States.
3. The doctor has just returned from a trip to regions of Wyoming and Colorado.
4. On her visit, this expert studied the foxes of the Rocky Mountains.
5. Her partner, David Anderson, took pages of careful notes.
6. The reporter Donna Chaney hoped to photograph the animals.
7. Lee lives in the city of Seattle.
8. The name of her company is Fox Watch.
9. Lee and Anderson will write an article together and give interviews.
10. In a few months, the researchers will travel to Mexico to continue their work.

For additional practice, turn to pages 186–187.

Writing Application

Use common and proper nouns to write about an animal study you'd like to take part in.

NOUNS

People's titles, names of holidays, days of the week, and months are also proper nouns. The important words in these nouns are capitalized.

Uncle Al	**Monday**	**March**	**Veterans Day**
Miss Rosen	**Tuesday**	**April**	**Thanksgiving**

Exercise 12

Find the proper nouns in these sentences. Tell where capital letters belong.

1. I spent the summer on aunt hemmy's ranch.
2. I went on sunday, june 12, and stayed two months.
3. I learned how to swim from uncle lew.
4. The brown family lives near whitefish, montana.
5. We went to a rodeo on the fourth of july.

For additional practice, turn to pages 188–189.

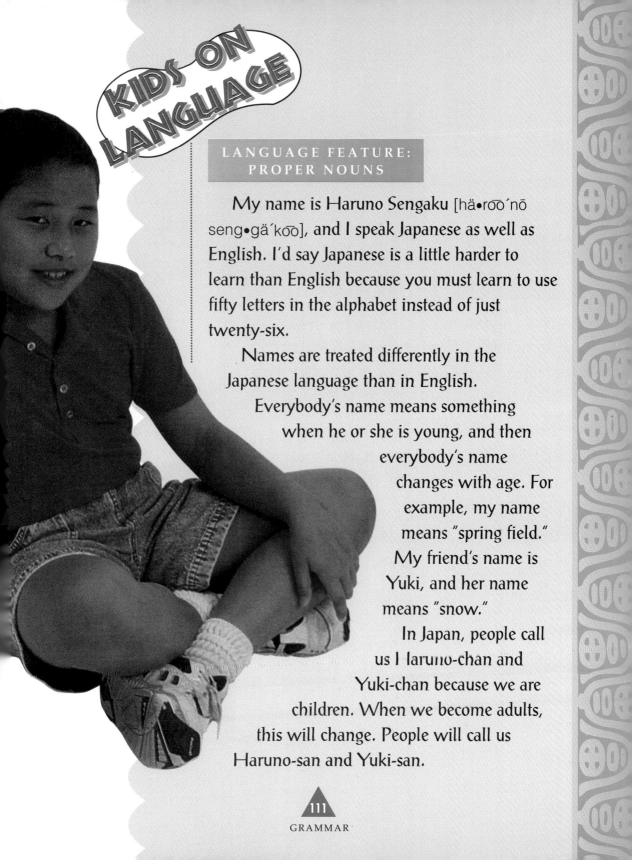

KIDS ON LANGUAGE

My name is Haruno Sengaku [hä•rōō´nō seng•gä´kōō], and I speak Japanese as well as English. I'd say Japanese is a little harder to learn than English because you must learn to use fifty letters in the alphabet instead of just twenty-six.

Names are treated differently in the Japanese language than in English. Everybody's name means something when he or she is young, and then everybody's name changes with age. For example, my name means "spring field." My friend's name is Yuki, and her name means "snow."

In Japan, people call us Haruno-chan and Yuki-chan because we are children. When we become adults, this will change. People will call us Haruno-san and Yuki-san.

NOUNS

SINGULAR NOUN

A *singular noun* names one person, place, or thing.

explorer   **marsh**   **sky**

PLURAL NOUN

A *plural noun* names more than one person, place, or thing. Make most nouns plural by adding *s* or *es*. If a noun ends in *y*, replace the *y* with an *i* and add *es* to form the plural.

explorers   **marshes**   **skies**

Some nouns change spelling in the plural form. Other nouns have the same singular and plural form.

Change Spelling	Same Singular and Plural
man–men	salmon
mouse–mice	elk
goose–geese	deer
wolf–wolves	trout

Exercise 13

Complete each sentence by giving the plural form of each noun in parentheses ( ).

1. Many (animal) travel in groups.
2. Monarch (butterfly) travel in swarms of a million or more.
3. Each year these (insect) migrate.
4. (Salmon) also travel in groups.
5. These fish hatch in (river).
6. They spend most of their (life) roaming the ocean.
7. Salmon find their way back to the rivers where they hatched to lay their own (egg).
8. Canadian (goose) are famous for their long yearly journey.
9. Each autumn, birds flying south for the winter are heard in the (sky).
10. Rocky Mountain bighorn (sheep) live and travel together in small herds.

For additional practice, turn to pages 190–191.

Writing Application

Use singular and plural nouns to describe a group of animals you have seen or read about.

NOUNS

A *possessive noun* shows ownership. It tells what someone or something owns or has.

a *flower's* stem
> The word flower's *tells that the stem belongs to the flower.*

the *scientists'* discoveries
> The word scientists' *tells that the discoveries belong to the scientists.*

Exercise 14

Identify each possessive noun. Then tell what belongs to that person or thing.

1. An insect's life can be dangerous.
2. The bug's search for food takes it from plant to plant.
3. The flytrap's sticky center attracts the fly.
4. Are you aware that a fly's sense of taste is in its feet?
5. When the prey lands, the plant's sides shut.
6. The leaf's spines close together.
7. A bee's life also has its danger.
8. This creature's search leads to the sundew.

For additional practice, turn to pages 192–193.

SINGULAR POSSESSIVE NOUN

A *singular possessive noun* shows ownership by one person or thing. To form the possessive of most singular nouns, add an apostrophe (') and *s*.

Jan Kinoki's report is about the timber wolf.

A *wolf's* keen vision and hearing help it hunt.

PLURAL POSSESSIVE NOUN

A *plural possessive noun* shows ownership by more than one person or thing. To form the possessive of a plural noun that ends in *s*, add an apostrophe ('). Add *'s* to plural nouns that do not end in *s*.

The *animals'* population has become small.

People's interest in wolves has grown.

Writing Application

Use possessive nouns to write about a wild animal that interests you.

115

NOUNS

POSSESSIVE NOUNS

Exercise 15

Find the possessive noun in each sentence.
Tell whether it is singular or plural.

1. Most dogs' legs are shorter than the legs of a wolf.

2. Many animals' feet are smaller, too.

3. A wolf's head is wider than the head of a German shepherd.

4. Some people's dislike of wolves is well known.

5. A rancher's sheep are often threatened by wolves.

6. Have you heard the saying "a wolf in sheep's clothing"?

7. A sick elk's slowness can make it a target.

8. These hunters' goal is only to find food.

For additional practice, turn to pages 194–195.

For additional practice, turn to pages 194–195.

PRONOUNS

A *pronoun* is a word that takes the place of one or more nouns. Some common pronouns are *I, me, you, he, him, we, us, she, her, it, they,* and *them.*

Raul received an unusual plant.

***He* brought *it* a supply of socks.**

> He *takes the place of* Raul. It *takes the place of* plant.

Exercise 16

Find the pronouns in these sentences. Tell which noun or nouns each pronoun replaces.

1. Raul's friend D.J. visited him.
2. He thought the plant looked weird.
3. "Wow, it is huge!" D.J. exclaimed.
4. "I fced it every day," Raul replied.
5. "You should see the plant eat," he added.

For additional practice, turn to pages 196–197.

For additional practice, turn to pages 196–197.

Writing Application

Describe an unusual plant you have seen.

Use some pronouns in your description.

PRONOUNS

A *subject pronoun* takes the place of one or more nouns in the subject of a sentence. The words *I, you, he, she, it, we,* and *they* are subject pronouns. Always capitalize the pronoun *I*.

I have a friend named Hal.

He likes to grow things.

You can always find my sister.

She is looking at Hal's plants.

They have won many prizes.

Subject pronouns are often used in contractions. A **contraction** is two words joined together with an apostrophe (') taking the place of one or more letters.

Soon, *I'm* going to the county fair with my neighbors.

We'll visit the Hall of Flowers.

You've never seen such roses!

They're the size of cabbages.

OBJECT PRONOUN

An *object pronoun* follows an action verb, such as *see* or *tell*, or a word called a **preposition**, such as *at, for, to,* or *with*. The object pronouns are *me, you, him, her, it, us,* and *them*.

We asked *him* to work to preserve the forests.

The governor sent *them* a helpful reply.

That was an important letter for *us*.

Exercise 17

Read each pair of sentences. Find each pronoun. Then tell whether it is a subject pronoun or an object pronoun.

1. Show me that book about world forests. I will share it with you.

2. Forest animals eat plants. They also eat seeds.

3. That squirrel has an acorn. Will the squirrel share it?

4. Where do a flowering plant's seeds come from? You can usually find them in the fruit.

5. Evergreen seeds are inside the cones. The ranger gave them to us.

For additional practice, turn to pages 198–199.

Writing Application

Describe an animal or animals you have observed in nature. Use subject pronouns and object pronouns in your description.

PRONOUNS

POSSESSIVE PRONOUN

A *possessive pronoun* shows ownership and takes the place of a possessive noun. There are two kinds of possessive pronouns. One kind is used before a noun. These pronouns are *my, your, his, her, its, our,* and *their.*

Pat's mom gave me a plant. *His* mom is nice.
> His *takes the place of* Pat's.

The other kind of possessive pronoun stands alone. These pronouns are *mine, yours, his, hers, ours,* and *theirs.*

This book is Kim's. I know it is *hers.*

Exercise 18

Identify each possessive pronoun.

1. Animals use their color to hide.
2. The chameleon's color changes are its defense.
3. Our plants use coloring, too.
4. Insects fly to their flowers.
5. Those lilies are mine.

For additional practice, turn to pages 200–201.

Kids on Language

My name is Eyanira Duverge [ā•yə•nē´rə dü•verzh´]. As a bilingual speaker, I have to switch back and forth between two languages, English and Spanish. There are a couple of things that I've noticed about doing that.

Sometimes in English, the words seem to go backwards. For example, *el gato de Angel* becomes *Angel's cat*. In Spanish, the cat comes first, which makes sense to me. In English, the name of the cat's owner comes first.

I've also noticed that I sometimes need more words to say something in Spanish than in English, even with possessive pronouns. Look at a similar example: *el gato de él*, which means "his cat." I usually use two words in English to describe that cat.

ADJECTIVES

ADJECTIVE

An *adjective* is a word that describes a noun or a pronoun. Adjectives may tell *what kind, how many*, or *which one*. An adjective can come before the noun it describes, or it can follow a linking verb, such as *is, seems*, or *appears*.

Large reefs are made of *four hundred* species of coral.

Currents are *warm*.

ARTICLE

The adjectives *a, an*, and *the* are called *articles.* The article *the* refers to a specific person, place, thing, or idea. The articles *a* and *an* refer to any person, place, thing, or idea.

Use *a* before a word that begins with a consonant sound. Use *an* before a word that begins with a vowel sound.

The climate in most of Australia is hot and dry.

A gum tree can still grow several hundred feet tall.

I wonder how much it grows in *an* hour.

An orchid in Australia grew to forty-nine feet.

122

Exercise 19

Find the adjectives and articles in these sentences.

1. The ocean has large and small animals.
2. Animals can live in the deep parts.
3. For an animal with a light shell, moving is easy.
4. Beautiful corals are fixed to the bottom in one position for life.
5. Plants do not live in the deep, dark waters of an ocean.
6. Seaweed grows in the shallow waters.
7. The giant kelp is a large kind of seaweed.
8. It can have a length of seventy feet!
9. Many kinds of bushy seaweeds grow over rocks.
10. The rocks are covered by water at high tide.

For additional practice, turn to pages 202–203.

Writing Application

Write a story about a trip to a faraway place with unusual plants. Use colorful adjectives.

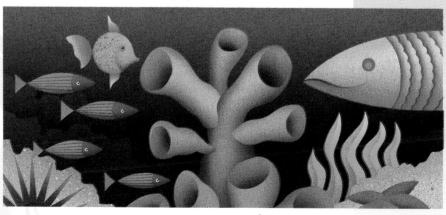

ADJECTIVES

Adjectives can describe by comparing people, places, or things. Add *-er* to most adjectives to compare two things. Add *-est* to most adjectives to compare more than two things.

Hank is a *fast* runner.

Lydia is *faster* than Hank.

Jacki is the *fastest* runner in Farmer County.

I grew some *pretty* tomatoes.

Your tomatoes are *prettier* than mine.

Brian has the *prettiest* tomatoes.

Exercise 20

In these sentences, find the words that compare. Tell who or what is being compared.

1. The fourth grade is having the biggest harvest carnival ever.
2. The field is bigger than last year's location.
3. The carnival is also noisier than last year's because there is music.
4. The string band plays the liveliest songs of any band.
5. The contest booths are sillier than last year's.
6. The person who makes the funniest face wins a prize.
7. Mr. Rourke baked the greatest cherry pie I ever tasted.
8. Mrs. Fernandez baked a larger pie than Mr. Rourke's.
9. The largest pie weighs ten pounds.
10. The fastest pie eater wins a baseball cap.

For additional practice, turn to pages 204–205.

For additional practice, turn to pages 204–205.

Writing Application

Write about a carnival or contest. Use adjectives ending in -er and -est to describe people and events.

ADJECTIVES

More and *most* are used with some adjectives to make comparisons. Use *more* with adjectives to compare two things. Use *most* with adjectives to compare more than two things.

The new dairy farm in East Haven is *more* modern than the old one.

The farms in the United States are among the *most* productive in all the world.

Exercise 21

Complete each sentence by adding *more* or *most*.

1. Don was _____ excited than Dani.
2. Dani was _____ excited than Ricky.
3. The _____ excited person of all was Denton.
4. The new dairy farm was even _____ beautiful than the new shopping mall.
5. The new dairy farm was the _____ wonderful thing ever to happen in East Haven!

For additional practice, turn to pages 206–207.

SPECIAL FORMS FOR COMPARING

Some adjectives have special forms for comparing.

Adjective	Comparing Two Things	Comparing More Than Two Things
good	better	best
bad	worse	worst

Exercise 22

Complete each sentence, using one of the words in parentheses ( ).

1. Mark has a (good/best) vegetable garden.
2. Stacy's is (good/better) than Mark's.
3. Mrs. Fong has the (good/best) garden of all.
4. "The (worse/worst) thing you can do is get discouraged," Mrs. Fong said.
5. "You'll do (good/better) than last year."

For additional practice, turn to pages 208–209.

For additional practice, turn to pages 208–209.

Writing Application

Write about a time when you improved at something. Use the words in the chart.

VERBS

A *verb* expresses action or being. The main word in the predicate of a sentence is the verb. The verb should agree in number with the subject.

People all over the world *play* board games.

They *compete* for fun and prizes.

The game of checkers *is* more than 700 years old.

Other games *are* even older.

Exercise 23

Tell what the verb is in each sentence.

1. The French probably invented the game of checkers.
2. Long ago, people carved the pieces from bone.
3. Most checkerboards have 64 squares.
4. The game board for Polish checkers has 100 squares.
5. The board for Chinese checkers forms a star shape.
6. Chinese checkers probably came from Europe.

For additional practice, turn to pages 210–211.

ACTION VERB

An *action verb* is a word that tells what the subject of a sentence does or did. Use strong action verbs to paint clear and vivid pictures.

A player *races* across an open field.

The crowd *cheered*.

Exercise 24

Find the action verb in each sentence.

1. The Tarahumara people of Mexico play a kind of kickball.
2. They make a ball from foil and rubber bands.
3. Each team chases its own ball.
4. One player tosses the ball high.
5. Then the players run after the ball.
6. Most players wear a sandal on one foot.
7. They kick the ball with their bare foot.
8. The teams race for up to forty miles!

For additional practice, turn to pages 212–213.

Writing Application

Use action verbs to describe a fast-moving game you know how to play.

VERBS

A *linking verb* connects the subject of a sentence to one or more words in the predicate. The most common linking verbs are forms of *be*. Some forms of *be* are *am, is, are, was,* and *were*. Some other common linking verbs are *become, feel,* and *seem*.

Duane and Aisha *are* in the backyard.

They *seem* happy about something.

Exercise 25

For each sentence, tell whether the verb is an action verb or a linking verb.

1. My brother Duane is creative.
2. Duane built a volcano model this afternoon.
3. His friend Aisha became an inventor.
4. She created an eruption inside the volcano!
5. Inventions are a hobby for Aisha and Duane.

For additional practice, turn to pages 214–215.

MAIN VERB

Sometimes a simple predicate is made up of two or more verbs. The *main verb* is the most important verb in the predicate. It comes last in a group of verbs.

People around the world <u>have</u> *played* board games for years.

We <u>are</u> *learning* games from many countries.

Exercise 26

Find the verbs in each sentence. Tell which is the main verb.

1. People in India are playing "Snakes and Ladders."
2. They have made a game board with 100 squares.
3. They are throwing dice.
4. Europeans had invented the game of "Goose" long ago.
5. They had added pictures of a goose to the board.

For additional practice, turn to pages 216–217.

For additional practice, turn to pages 216–217.

Writing Application

Describe how your favorite board game is played. With a partner, discuss the main verbs you use.

VERBS

HELPING VERB

A *helping verb* can work with the main verb to tell about an action. The helping verb always comes before the main verb. These words are often used as helping verbs:

| am | is | are | was | were |

| has | have | had | will |

Our class *is* organizing a large picnic.

We *will* invite our friends and families.

We *have* organized picnics before.

This time we *will* plan unusual games.

Sometimes another word comes between a main verb and a helping verb.

We *have* just learned how to play a new game.

The class *will* certainly have a lot to do!

Exercise 27

Find the verbs in each sentence. Tell which word is the helping verb.

1. Mr. and Mrs. Ames have invited us to their farm.
2. We are planning a game.
3. Mrs. Chu is helping us.
4. We will play a game of "Mud Tug."
5. Mr. Ames has made a huge mud puddle near the cornfield.
6. Two teams will tug on a rope.
7. One unlucky team will probably fall into the mud.
8. At first Mrs. Chu had said no to "Mud Tug."
9. She had worried about the mess.
10. Everyone will bring a change of clothes.

For additional practice, turn to pages 218–219.

Writing Application

Use sentences with helping verbs to describe an unusual game you know about or have played. Share your description.

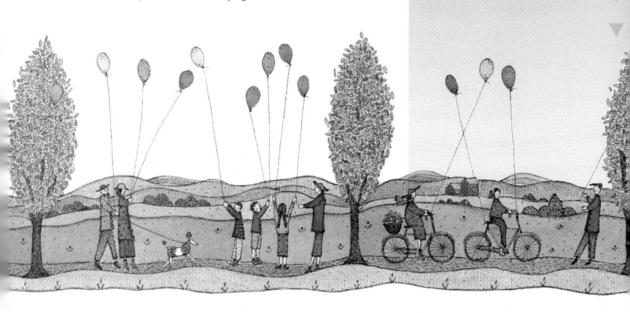

VERBS

The *tense* of a verb shows when the action happens.

Today corn *is* the most important crop grown in our country. PRESENT

Native Americans first *grew* corn thousands of years ago. PAST

This afternoon we *will watch* a filmstrip about corn. FUTURE

Exercise 28

Read each sentence and tell whether it describes an action in the past, the present, or the future.

1. Today Carla visits a Mexican market.
2. She buys fresh tortillas.
3. Later she will add meat and cheese.
4. Carla's family enjoyed her meal.
5. In the past, people made tortillas by hand.
6. Today machines make tortillas, too.
7. Carla will make tamales tomorrow.

KIDS ON LANGUAGE

My name is Tessie Carroll. I am an American who was born in the Philippine Islands in Southeast Asia. Tagalog [tə•gä´log] is the language that is spoken there. Tagalog has many words that come from the Spanish language, such as *grado* (grade) and *clase* (class). But Tagalog has its own rules, and they are very different from the rules of either Spanish or English.

One of the biggest differences between Tagalog and these other languages is the verb *be*. There is no such verb in Tagalog. Let me show you what I mean.

To say *I am American* in Spanish, you say *Yo (I) soy (am) americana*. You can't do that in Tagalog. You say *Americana akó*. There is a word for *I* and a word for *American*, but there is no word for the verb!

VERBS

A verb in the *present tense* shows action that is happening now or happens over and over. Add *s* or *es* to most present-tense verbs when the subject is *he, she, it,* or a singular noun. Do not add *s* or *es* with *I, you, we, they,* or a plural noun.

Maria's family *grows* coffee beans.

She *watches* the harvest.

The beans *grow* on bushes.

Exercise 29

Choose the correct verb in parentheses ( ) to complete each sentence.

1. Workers (pick/picks) coffee berries.
2. A berry (contain/contains) two beans.
3. Each picker (wash/washes) berries.
4. A machine (separate/separates) the beans.

For additional practice, turn to pages 220–221.

PAST TENSE

A verb in the *past tense* shows action that happened in the past. Add *ed* or *d* to most verbs to form the past tense.

Twelve thousand years ago, hunters *followed* herds into what is now Mexico.

They *hunted* huge mammoths.

These gigantic mammals *died* long ago.

Exercise 30

Tell which verb in parentheses ( ) correctly completes each sentence.

1. Last year my family (visit/visited) Mayan pyramids in Mexico.
2. The Maya (thrives/thrived) around A.D. 250–900.
3. The Maya (created/create) huge pyramids out of limestone.
4. They (develop/developed) a writing system.
5. Artists (paints/painted) murals on walls.
6. The Maya (charts/charted) the star movements.

For additional practice, turn to pages 222–223.

For additional practice, turn to pages 222–223.

Writing Application

Write about an interesting place you have visited. Use present-tense and past-tense verbs.

VERBS

An *irregular verb* does not end with *ed* in the past tense. Some irregular verbs show past time by using a different form of the main verb with *have, has,* or *had.* Here are some irregular verbs.

Present	Past	Past with Helping Verb
come, comes	came	(have, has, had) come
do, does	did	(have, has, had) done
drive, drives	drove	(have, has, had) driven
eat, eats	ate	(have, has, had) eaten
give, gives	gave	(have, has, had) given
go, goes	went	(have, has, had) gone
have, has	had	(have, has, had) had
ride, rides	rode	(have, has, had) ridden
run, runs	ran	(have, has, had) run
say, says	said	(have, has, had) said
see, sees	saw	(have, has, had) seen
take, takes	took	(have, has, had) taken
think, thinks	thought	(have, has, had) thought

Exercise 31

Choose the correct verb in parentheses ( ) to complete each sentence.

1. Today we (seen/saw) a video on the world's animals.
2. I (thought/thinks) the animals from Mexico were neat.
3. I knew Mexico (give/gave) us Chihuahuas.
4. The guide (rode/ridden) through mountains, pointing out bears, deer, and mountain lions.
5. The northern deserts (had/has) coyotes and prairie dogs.
6. I would have (run/ran) from the rattlesnakes.
7. Next, the guide (go/went) to the southern forests to show us colorful birds.
8. Then he (drove/driven) to the coast.
9. I didn't know many shrimp (came/has come) from Mexico!
10. Tuna fish is another of their products I have (ate/eaten).

For additional practice, turn to pages 224–225.

Writing Application

Use some of the words in the chart to write about the most interesting animal you have ever seen.

VERBS

A verb in the *future tense* shows action that will happen in the future. To form the future tense of a verb, use the helping verb *will* with the main verb.

Tomorrow we *will visit* my aunt's new restaurant.

The cook *will make* my favorite tamales for dinner.

Exercise 32
Choose the future-tense verb to complete each sentence.

1. First, the cook (will steam/steamed) the corn meal.

2. Then he (chop/will chop) some chicken into pieces.

3. His assistant (will mix/mix) it with herbs and spices.

4. Finally, he (will put/had put) the tamales together.

5. We (will have/having) frijoles, too.

For additional practice, turn to pages 226–227.

ADVERERBS

ADVERB

An **adverb** is a word that describes a verb. An adverb may tell *when, where,* or *how* an action happens. Adverbs that tell *how* often end in *ly*.

The Kleins visited Belle Isle Park on the Detroit River *today*. WHEN

They saw many interesting things *there*. WHERE

The family drove *slowly* through the park. HOW

Exercise 33

Name each adverb. Tell whether it says *where, when,* or *how* an action happens.

1. The family walked excitedly into the aquarium building.
2. They looked around for large fish.
3. Their son eagerly pointed at one.
4. Later they saw deer at the children's zoo.
5. Then a speaker gave a talk about Michigan's history and animals.

For additional practice, turn to pages 228–229.

Writing Application

Describe an outing you enjoyed. Use some adverbs.

ADVERBS

ADVERBS THAT COMPARE

Adverbs can be used to compare two or more actions. When you compare two actions, add *-er* to most short adverbs. For more than two actions, add *-est*.

Jeremy jumped out of the wagon *faster* than Erin.

Why did Jeremy jump out *fastest* of all the children?

Use *more* and *most* before adverbs that have two or more syllables.

Jeremy ran *more eagerly* than Erin.

He looked *most eagerly* at the store's mints.

Exercise 34

Tell which word or group of words in parentheses ( ) correctly completes each sentence.

1. Of all places in the country, the frontier towns were growing the (quickly/most quickly).

2. Trains arrived there (faster/fastest) than horses.

3. Goods were unloaded (more rapidly/rapider) from horses, though.

4. Some families waited (more patiently/most patiently) than other families.

5. The wares in the store sold (better/most good) than in the past.

6. People shopped (more carefully/carefuller) in winter than in summer.

7. Winter would come (earlier/early) this year than last year.

8. The children looked (attentive/more attentively) at the peppermints than at the flour or butter.

For additional practice, turn to pages 230–231.

Writing Application

Write a paragraph comparing today to long ago. Use adverbs to make the comparison.

NEGATIVES

A word that means "no" is called a *negative*. The words *never, no, nobody, none, not, nothing,* and *nowhere* are negatives.

Joe had *never* worked in a factory before.

Nobody there knew him.

The negative word *not* is often used in a contraction.

He *didn't* know at first how hard the work was.

He *couldn't* sleep at night.

Exercise 35

Find the negative in each sentence.

1. No other factory owner worked the long hours Mr. Anderson did.
2. His furnaces churned out steel like nobody else's.
3. Railroad builders couldn't wait for the new steel.
4. Nowhere else did the mills pollute so quickly.
5. That owner did little or nothing to save natural resources.

For additional practice, turn to pages 232–233.

TROUBLESOME WORDS

Use *too* when you mean "more than enough" or "also."

Washington State is *too* beautiful for words!

Alaska is a great state, *too*.

Use *to* when you mean "in the direction of."

I've never been *to* the Northwest.

Use *two* when you mean the number.

My aunt and uncle went there for *two* weeks.

Exercise 36

Complete each sentence by choosing *too, to,* or *two.*

1. Long ago, the Kwakiutl people came _____ the Northwest.
2. The Kwakiutl were friends _____ the wilderness.
3. No _____ of their beautiful masks look alike.
4. The masks were never worn _____ daily events.
5. The masks seem _____ heavy to me.

For additional practice, turn to pages 234–235.

Writing Application

Describe two interesting crafted objects you have seen. Use too, two, *and* to.

TROUBLESOME WORDS

GOOD, WELL

The word *good* is an adjective. It describes a noun.

Ari's idea is *good*.

We should do a *good* deed for the town.

The word *well* is an adverb. It tells more about a verb.

Everyone in this family works together *well*.

Ari plans projects *well*.

Exercise 37

Tell whether to use *good* or *well*.

1. Ari and Elise are _____ cooks.
2. Their special flat bread is always _____.
3. It sold _____ at last year's fair.
4. It was Ari's _____ idea to buy three small trees with the money.
5. Ari researched the topic _____.
6. The trees were a _____ choice.
7. We prepared _____ for our planting project.
8. The trees are a _____ addition to West Street!

For additional practice, turn to pages 236–237.

Use **they're** when you mean "they are."

They're small, silver, and smart.

They're robots!

Use **their** when you mean "belonging to them."

Their "brains" are really computers.

Use **there** when you mean "in that place."

I like that little robot over *there*.

Exercise 38

Choose the correct word in parentheses ( ) to complete each sentence.

1. Robots are loyal to (they're/their) owners.
2. (Their/They're) good to have nearby.
3. That one over (there/their) has been in the family for years.
4. (Their/They're) the perfect helpers.
5. Robots are worth (their/they're) weight in metal.

For additional practice, turn to pages 238–239.

Writing Application

Write about a family tradition you know of and enjoy. Use good, well, they're, their, *and* there *in your writing.*

TROUBLESOME WORDS

IT'S, ITS

Use *it's* when you mean "it is."

It's a good day to carve a totem pole.

My uncle Mike says it's easy to do.

Use *its* when you mean "belonging to it."

A totem pole has many figures on its body.

Its colors are eye-catching.

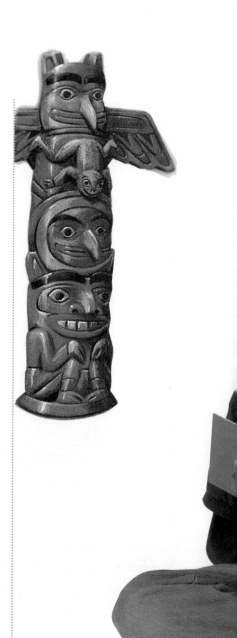

Exercise 39

Use *it's* or *its* to complete each sentence.

1. _____ morning when Uncle Mike gets started.
2. When I see the log, _____ size surprises me.
3. _____ huge and heavy.
4. Small knots cover _____ surface.
5. I try to carve a bird, but _____ not very good.
6. _____ wings look funny.
7. _____ important to be patient.

For additional practice, turn to pages 240–241.

Kids on Language

My name is Jean Edmond [jēn əd•môɲ]. I am from Haiti, where most people speak two languages! In school, subjects are taught in French, the official language of Haiti. But during recess, students speak Creole, the popular language.

French and Creole have many words that are the same, but there are different words and different rules, too. You have to be careful not to get things mixed up!

For example, in English you say *the street* (singular) and *the streets* (plural). The word *the* stays the same. In French and Creole, the word *the* changes with the singular and plural. In French, you say *la rue* (singular) and *les rues* (plural). In Creole, you say *ru-la* and *ru-yo*. The article, which is placed behind the noun, changes from *-la* to *-yo*.

149

TROUBLESOME WORDS

YOU'RE, YOUR

Use *you're* when you mean "you are."

You're welcome to join our quilting group.

You're doing such beautiful work!

Use *your* when you mean "belonging to you."

Did *your* grandmother pass on this tradition?

Don't forget to bring *your* sketches next week.

Exercise 40

Choose *your* or *you're* to complete each sentence. Then explain your choice.

1. Randy tells me _____ interested in different crafts.
2. Is _____ brother this talented, too?
3. I hear _____ also a good nature artist.
4. Did _____ family teach you how to do this?
5. Allen says _____ making a quilt.

For additional practice, turn to pages 242–243.

COMMAS

Use a *comma* after each item except the last one in a series of three or more items.

Many cities are threatened by air pollution, water pollution, and litter.

Schools, businesses, and individuals can help.

Exercise 41

Tell where commas belong in each sentence.

1. People can use their cars trucks or motorcycles less.
2. They can go to the store the cleaners and the post office in one trip.
3. Individuals can also walk skate or ride a bike.
4. Families can conserve water gas and electricity.
5. Plastic aluminum and glass can be recycled.

For additional practice, turn to pages 244–245.

Writing Application

Describe several things you can do to help the environment. Use commas to separate items in a series.

COMMAS

Use a comma to set off the words *yes, no,* and *well* at the beginning of a sentence.

Yes, I have visited the river.

No, we didn't hunt the animals.

Well, we did photograph a rabbit.

Use a comma to set off the name of a person spoken to directly in a sentence.

Mario, may I use your pole?

Reel in that beautiful trout, Jim!

Exercise 42

Tell where commas go.

1. **Thea is this fishing line yours?**
2. **No it belongs to Angela.**
3. **What an amazing catch Marcus!**
4. **Yes this is the best fishing spot.**

For additional practice, turn to pages 246–247.

QUOTATIONS

DIALOGUE AND DIRECT QUOTATIONS

Use *quotation marks* (" ") before and after a direct quotation. To decide how to place quotation marks in dialogue and how to use quotation marks with other punctuation marks, use these examples as models.

Kesara asked, "May I see your blanket?"

"Look at the beautiful needlework!" she cried.

"I made it myself," said Soji.

Exercise 43

Read the sentences. Tell where the quotation marks belong in each sentence.

1. I need a book for our lesson on Africa, said Jon.
2. How about this one? asked the librarian.
3. It has beautiful pictures, she continued.
4. Jon gasped, Wow, look at that waterfall!
5. Many people want to visit Victoria Falls, she said.

For additional practice, turn to pages 248–249.

For additional practice, turn to pages 248–249.

Writing Application

Write a dialogue in which you and a friend tell about an amazing natural wonder you have seen. Use commas and quotation marks correctly.

TITLES

TITLES

Capitalize the first word, the last word, and all the important words in a *title*.

My favorite song is "Take Me Out to the Ball Game."

Underline the title of a book, a magazine, a newspaper, a movie, or a television show.

I liked the book <u>Minor League Heroes</u>.

Use quotation marks before and after the title of a story, a poem, or a song.

My favorite story is "Against All Odds."

Exercise 44

Tell how each title should appear.

1. I'm reading a book called big leagues.
2. The story I remember is the strikeout.
3. I wrote a poem called baseball.
4. My poem was in today magazine.
5. Our class learned a song called you've got to have heart.
6. I watch the weekly television show called bases.

For additional practice, turn to pages 250–251.

ABBREVIATIONS

ABBREVIATIONS

An *abbreviation* is a short way to write a word. Use a period after most abbreviations. Capitalize abbreviations that stand for proper nouns.

Dr. A. J. Mackenzi (Doctor Anita Jane Mackenzi)

336 W. Oak St. (336 West Oak Street)

Wed., Aug. 5 (Wednesday, August 5)

U.S. (United States)

Exercise 45

Tell how you could write each underlined word or group of words using abbreviations.

1. Randy lives on Elm Avenue in New York.
2. His pen pal, Maria Elena Gomez, is a native of Argentina.
3. Mister Alonzo Gomez owns a ranch.
4. Maria helps the gauchos during August.
5. Maria wants to visit the United States in the future.
6. Randy writes his friend every Tuesday.

For additional practice, turn to pages 252–253.

Writing Application

Write a list showing titles of movies, shows, or books and when you plan to see or read each. Use abbreviations of months or days, and be sure to write titles correctly.

Kids on Language

Hi! My name is Kunal Saigal [kōō•näl´ sā•gəl], and many of my family members speak Hindi as well as English. Hindi is the language spoken by millions of people in India. It is a very old language.

In Hindi, it is very important to call a person by the correct title. It is a sign of respect. It is far more complicated to get someone's title right in Hindi than in English.

In English I call all of my uncles the same thing—*Uncle*. In Hindi, different types of uncles get different titles. For example, my father's older brothers are called *Thau*. My father's younger brothers are called *Chacha*.

Handwriting

Handwriting

Handwriting Tips

Using correct posture, writing grip, and paper position can help you write clearly. These tips will help you get ready for writing. See pages 159–164 for tips to help you form letters and words.

Posture

- Sit up straight, with both feet on the floor. Your hips should be toward the back of the chair. Lean forward slightly, but don't slouch.

Paper Position

- Slant the paper toward the elbow of your writing arm. Hold the top corner of the paper with your other hand.

Writing Grip

- Hold your pen or pencil about an inch from the point. Hold it between your thumb and pointer finger. Rest it on your middle finger. Let your other fingers curve under.

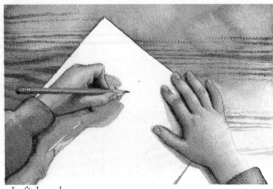

Left-hander

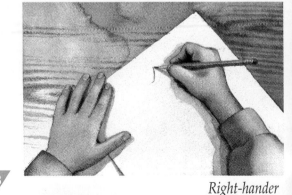

Right-hander

Uppercase and Lowercase Manuscript Alphabet

A B C D E F G H I

J K L M N O P Q R

S T U V W X Y Z

a b c d e f g h i

j k l m n o p q r

s t u v w x y z

A B C D E F G H I

J K L M N O P Q R

S T U V W X Y Z

a b c d e f g h i

j k l m n o p q r

s t u v w x y z

A B C D E F G H I
J K L M N O P Q R
S T U V W X Y Z
a b c d e f g h i
j k l m n o p q r
s t u v w x y z

A B C D E F G H I
J K L M N O P Q R
S T U V W X Y Z
a b c d e f g h i
j k l m n o p q r
s t u v w x y z

Elements of Handwriting

Shape

Write each letter using the correct shape.

correct

Friday

incorrect

Friday

Spacing of Letters

Space letters properly so that they are easy to read.

not enough space between letters

house

correct spacing

house

too much space between letters

house

Spacing of Words and Sentences

This is a spacer: ☐ It is about the width of your pencil or pen. Leave room for one spacer between words and one spacer after end punctuation. Leave room for two spacers at the beginning of each paragraph.

Position

All letters should sit evenly on the bottom line.

correct

evenly

incorrect

evenly

Size

Tall letters fill one full space. Most short letters fill one half-space above the bottom line. Most tail letters fill one half-space above and one half-space below the bottom line.

correct

hobby

incorrect

hobby

Slant

Slant your letters in the same direction to make your writing easy to read.

correct

mark

incorrect

mark

Stroke

Keep your letter strokes smooth and steady. Do not mark over strokes you have already written. The letters should not be too light or too dark.

correct

eat

unsteady

eat

too light

eat

too dark

eat

incorrect | correct

Touch the top line.
The **l** could look like **e**.

incorrect | correct

Be sure the joining stroke is long enough. The **wr** could look like **ur**.

incorrect | correct

Close the letter **a**.
The **a** could look like **u**.

incorrect | correct

Keep the joining stroke high.
The **o** could look like **a**.

incorrect | correct

Use the overcurve stroke.
The **k** could look like **t**.

incorrect | correct

Bring the down stroke to the bottom line. Then make an undercurve. The **un** could look like **vn**.

incorrect   correct

Make your final stroke a straight slant. The **h** could look like **k**.

incorrect   correct

Make a loop at the top and the bottom. The **f** could look like **j**.

incorrect   correct

Curve up and then down twice for **r**. The letters **or** could look like **oi**.

incorrect   correct

Use one overcurve joining stroke before forming the **n**. The **n** could look like **m**.

incorrect   correct

Use one overcurve joining stroke before forming the **m**. The **m** could look like **n**.

incorrect   correct

Begin the **u** with an undercurve. The **u** could look like **ri**.

ADDITIONAL PRACTICE

Grammar

Usage

Mechanics

SENTENCES

A. Read each group of words, and write whether it is a sentence.

Examples:

People do tricks with yo-yos.

sentence

Are very popular toys.

not a sentence

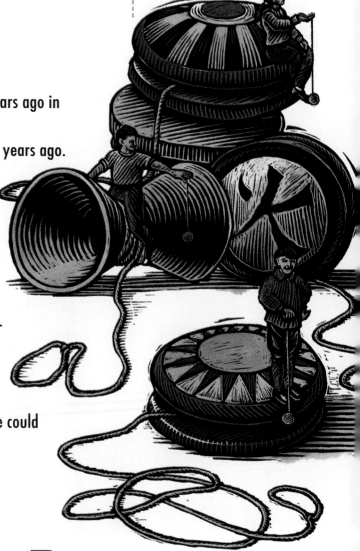

1. Yo-yos were invented 3,000 years ago in China.
2. Brought to Europe hundreds of years ago.
3. In England, this toy was called a *quiz*.
4. Popular in France, too.
5. In the Philippines, yo-yos were used for a serious purpose.
6. Hunters threw them at animals.
7. An American named Donald Duncan.
8. Duncan visited the Philippines.
9. He was amazed by what people could do with yo-yos.
10. Decided to make toy yo-yos.

B. Identify each sentence. Revise each of the other groups of words so it becomes a sentence.

Examples:

Lillian Leitzel performed on the flying trapeze.

> *sentence*

The first person in the Circus Hall of Fame.

> *She was the first person in the Circus Hall of Fame.*

11. Lillian was in a circus family.
12. Her mother was a trapeze artist.
13. Her grandmother was one, too.
14. At the age of 84 on the trapeze.
15. As a child Lillian played the piano well.
16. Dreamed of being a musician.
17. Instead, she joined the family act.
18. She came to this country at age 15.
19. She, her mother, and two aunts with the Barnum and Bailey Circus.
20. Lillian Leitzel developed new tricks.

DECLARATIVE AND INTERROGATIVE SENTENCES

A. Read the sentences, and identify each declarative sentence.

Examples:

Geologists study minerals.

declarative

Why is Monique so serious?

not declarative

1. Monique is hiking across the desert with her grandfather.
2. They are looking for minerals.
3. What is so special about that rock?
4. They will polish it into a smooth stone.
5. Shouldn't Monique choose an easier hobby?

B. Read the sentences, and identify each interrogative sentence.

6. Rocks are more than just her hobby.
7. She plans to become a geologist.
8. Where can she learn how to use scientific instruments to help her?
9. Will she attend the Colorado School of Mines?
10. Isn't that college in Golden?

C. Revise the sentences. Make each declarative sentence a question. Make each question a declarative sentence.

Example:
Kyle really did like the neighborhood talent show.

Did Kyle really like the neighborhood talent show?

11. Miss Merlin can do amazing tricks.

12. Were the tickets free?

13. The theater is crowded.

14. The audience was noisy.

15. Are the children getting restless?

16. Miss Merlin finally did appear.

17. Are those flowers painted in red glitter on her cape?

18. Is her act funny?

19. This is Kyle's favorite show.

20. Miss Merlin will pull a fake rabbit from an old hat.

EXCLAMATORY AND IMPERATIVE SENTENCES

A. Identify each exclamatory sentence.

Examples:

That cabin must be 100 years old!

　exclamatory

Look at this old bottle.

　not exclamatory

1. Ask if we can dig for old bottles.
2. She says we're welcome to search!
3. Dig slowly and carefully.
4. My shovel just struck something!
5. I may have found a treasure!

B. Identify each imperative sentence.

6. Put this old flowerpot in the trash.
7. Now you've uncovered something!
8. Bring me the water jug and a rag.
9. What a beautiful bottle this is!
10. Wrap it carefully for the ride home.

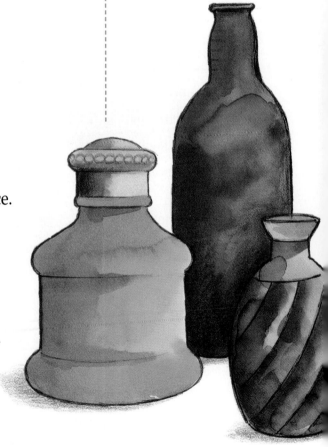

C. Read the sentences, and identify each one as an exclamation or a command.

Examples:

I've lost my new sunglasses!

exclamation

Help me look for them.

command

11. Please call my friend Jeremy.
12. Ask him to look in his basement.
13. Maybe I left my sunglasses at the park!
14. Ride my bicycle there, Mindy.
15. Dad gave them to me for my birthday!
16. Good sunglasses are expensive!
17. Check on top of Mom's computer.
18. I think I see them on the table!
19. Those are Grandma's!
20. What a disappointment!
21. Answer the telephone.
22. Jeremy has found a pair of sunglasses in his basement!
23. Please answer the door.
24. Mindy found a pair at the park!
25. They can't both be mine!

SIMPLE AND COMPOUND SENTENCES

A. Identify each simple sentence.

Example:

Kim is running for student council.

  simple sentence

1. Candidates will give speeches today.
2. Kim wrote a speech, and she has practiced it.
3. She feels a little nervous.
4. Antonio will speak first.
5. Lin has a plan for the school.

B. Identify each compound sentence.

Example:

The students might elect Lin, or they might vote for one of the others.

  compound sentence

6. Lin's speech is very funny.
7. Kim steps to the front of the room, and she trips over a book on the floor.
8. She opens her mouth, but no words come out.
9. Kim does not expect a victory, but she flashes a victory sign anyway.
10. Antonio wins, and Kim congratulates him.

C. Revise each pair of simple sentences so they become a compound sentence.

Example:

Dwight David Eisenhower was elected President in 1952. He was elected to a second term in 1956.

Dwight David Eisenhower was elected President in 1952, and he was elected to a second term in 1956.

11. Eisenhower was born in Texas. He soon moved to Kansas.

12. He was a good student. He was a fine football player in high school.

13. Dwight wanted a college education. His family had very little money.

14. He had one hope for a free education. That was the military.

15. The United States Military Academy chooses a few good students each year. It chose Dwight.

16. Dwight entered the academy. He got a fine education in exchange for service.

17. General Eisenhower led the army to victory during World War II. Seven years later he was elected President.

SUBJECTS AND PREDICATES

A. Write the subject of each sentence.

Example:

Many dogs compete in contests.
   Many dogs

1. Kenji throws the Frisbee high.
2. A small dog runs along under it.
3. The dog leaps high into the air.
4. He grabs the Frisbee with his teeth!
5. This talented dog is named Bo.

B. Write the predicate of each sentence.

Example:

Small dogs are often good jumpers.
   are often good jumpers

6. Bo is competing for a prize.
7. The crowd cheers loudly for Bo.
8. Kenji cheers, too.
9. Bo's final catch is the best one.
10. He wins the championship!

C. Identify the subject and the predicate in each sentence.

Example:
Harvey Ladew led an exciting life.
> *subject—Harvey Ladew*
> *predicate—led an exciting life*

11. New York State was his birthplace.
12. Harvey crossed Africa's desert in his youth.
13. He visited Paris, London, and other famous cities.
14. The traveler settled near Baltimore.
15. Mr. Ladew was a talented gardener.
16. His special skill turned plants into animals.
17. He trimmed bushes into the shapes of horses.
18. A long hedge became waves with swans.
19. A leafy rooster perched on a tree.
20. This skillful gardener created imaginary animals, too.
21. He turned a tree into a unicorn.
22. Ladew tended his garden for fifty years.

COMPLETE AND SIMPLE SUBJECTS

A. Read each sentence, and write the complete subject.

Example:

My little brother loses things.

My little brother

1. A big sister is a good detective.
2. This great detective knows all.
3. My best friend can find clues.
4. Our mother is getting impatient.
5. The swamp is the place to look.

B. Read each sentence, and write the simple subject.

Example:

The best clues are found here.

clues

6. The other kids were in the swamp.
7. The most brilliant detective would be proud of me.
8. I can show you the missing stone.
9. Your solution is not correct.
10. The stone is in my pocket!

C. Write the complete subject in each sentence. Underline the simple subject.

Example:

The rushing river calls to Grandpa and me.

   The rushing <u>river</u>

11. The shallow water is still and quiet.
12. My daring grandpa helps me put my life jacket on.
13. My favorite place is the front of the boat.
14. The other seat is for Grandpa.
15. That position is for steering.
16. Our steady course leads between rocks.
17. Two big fish jump in the river.
18. A good meal is important on a long ride.
19. The cool water splashes onto my lap.
20. My delicious sandwich is soaked.
21. A real adventurer doesn't mind.
22. My favorite person is my sporty grandpa.

COMPOUND SUBJECTS

A. Identify the compound subject in each sentence.

Example:

Your school and your community need your help!

Your school and your community

1. Parents and teachers often help.

2. Girls and boys can help, too.

3. Clubs and organizations need good officers.

4. Good presidents and vice presidents take charge.

5. A loud person or a popular student is not always the best leader.

6. Friendly classmates and helpful students get lots of votes.

7. Honesty and a polite manner count.

8. A friend or a family member can help with your campaign.

9. Your teachers and classmates will be glad you were elected.

10. Hard work and a good attitude pay.

B. Write each compound subject. Underline the word that joins the parts of the compound subject.

Example:
A carnival and a circus are planned.

   A carnival <u>and</u> a circus

11. Parents and children like circuses.

12. The gym or the field is the place to hold one.

13. Our teacher and the principal will take part.

14. Clowns and other performers will entertain our guests.

15. Both happy clowns and sad clowns are fun to watch.

16. Smiles or frowns are painted on their faces.

17. Makeup and silly clothes are all we need.

18. Lions and tigers are hard to get.

19. Mr. Dowling and his helpers will bring some ponies.

20. Balloons and streamers make the circus fun.

COMPLETE AND SIMPLE PREDICATES

A. Write each complete predicate.

Example:

Barney cheers up many patients.

cheers up many patients

1. This dog visits Valley Hospital.
2. He greets his friends with barks.
3. Mr. Fletcher shakes hands.
4. Jimmy teaches Barney tricks.
5. Evelyn feeds Barney pieces of bacon.

B. Write each simple predicate.

Example:

Phil scratches Barney's head.

scratches

6. A woman takes Barney for a walk.
7. Mr. Fong had an operation.
8. He missed Barney's visits.
9. This friendly man calls for Barney.
10. Barney licks his hand happily.

C. Read the sentences. Write the complete predicate in each sentence. Underline the simple predicate.

Example:
The cargo ship struck a huge rock far out in the Pacific Ocean.

<u>struck</u> a huge rock far out in the Pacific Ocean

11. The rock damaged the ship.
12. The crew grabbed life jackets.
13. They boarded the lifeboat quickly.
14. The crew members lowered it into the sea.
15. The captain started the engine.
16. The crew shook their heads sadly.
17. The cargo ship was beyond repair.
18. The lifeboat served them well, though.
19. People on shore sent rescue planes.
20. Several planes searched for the crew.
21. One had a pigeon aboard.
22. The bird spotted orange life jackets.
23. The plane took the crew to land.

COMPOUND PREDICATES

A. Write each compound predicate.

Example:
Dolphins leap and splash in the sea.

leap and splash in the sea

1. These mammals act playful and are intelligent.
2. They solve problems and communicate.
3. Dolphins find people and save their lives.
4. One legend is old and seems odd.
5. A sailor fell overboard and nearly drowned.
6. A dolphin circled around him and then swam up to him.
7. The sailor grabbed the dolphin and held on.
8. The dolphin brought him close to land and then pushed him toward shore.
9. The sailor swam to shore and told of his amazing rescue.
10. Other legends describe similar rescues and fascinate listeners.

B. Read the sentences. Write each compound predicate. Underline the word that joins its two parts.

Example:

Bloodhounds search for missing people and often find them.

search for missing people <u>and</u> often find them

11. A hiker loses sight of his group and tries to find his way back.

12. His friends call him and look all around.

13. The sheriff calls the search leader and then drives to the forest.

14. The search leader arrives and opens the back of her station wagon.

15. The sheriff asks for the hiker's jacket and holds it toward two dogs.

16. The hounds sniff the jacket and run quickly into the woods.

17. The dogs bark and whine as a signal.

18. The hiker laughs and pats the dogs.

19. Each hero gets a dog biscuit or receives another treat.

A. Read each sentence, and write the nouns.

Example:

The Arabic language gave us the name of that tall animal.

language, name, animal

1. The tallest mammal in the world is the giraffe.
2. Giraffes have long legs and necks.
3. These animals live on the plains.
4. These graceful creatures eat plants.
5. Giraffes eat leaves from the tops of trees.
6. This food is too high for other animals to reach.
7. Herds travel across the land.
8. Many animals visit wells in the morning and the evening.
9. This special group seldom drinks from streams or lakes.
10. Their water comes from the things they eat.

B. List each noun in the sentences below.

Example:

Scientists can tell the favorite food of a bird from the shape of its beak.

Scientists, food, bird, shape, beak

11. Hummingbirds sip nectar from plants.

12. These birds also eat insects and spiders.

13. The bugs are good sources of protein.

14. Toucans have large beaks.

15. Their bills reach fruit in prickly bushes.

16. Macaws have powerful jaws.

17. These parrots crack nuts with hard shells.

18. Visitors must keep their fingers away from the cage with this animal in it.

19. Hawks, falcons, and eagles catch prey in the daytime.

20. These divers can soar through the air.

COMMON AND PROPER NOUNS

A. Write the common nouns in each sentence.

Example:

Many coyotes roam the open prairies.

coyotes, prairies

1. Coyotes can live through the long, cold winters in the Rocky Mountains.
2. These animals often hunt in teams.
3. Even the pups have sharp eyes.
4. Adults may surround a large animal.
5. These hunters also eat fruit.

B. Write the proper noun in each sentence.

Example:

Coyotes live in the United States.

United States

6. Do they sing to the moon in Utah?
7. They do in California.
8. In Canada, coyotes stalk sheep.
9. The coat of the coyote protects it from harsh weather in Maine.
10. These animals like the heat of the Southwest.

C. Read the sentences. List all the nouns. Underline any proper nouns.

Example:

Snakes are found on every continent except Antarctica.

snakes, continent, <u>Antarctica</u>

11. The cobra lives in many parts of Asia.

12. Most mongooses live on that continent, too.

13. Rudyard Kipling wrote a story about these two animals.

14. Chameleons live in Europe, Africa, and Asia.

15. These lizards can change the color of their skin.

16. Scientists have discovered these reptiles do not change to blend into their surroundings.

17. My teacher says their color changes with their moods.

18. Many camels live in the Middle East.

19. The animals in the Sanford Zoo have their own areas.

MORE PROPER NOUNS

A. Read the sentences, and write each proper noun.

Example:

Explorers left Russia in 1741.

Russia

1. The leader was Vitus Bering, who was from Denmark.

2. Georg Wilhelm Steller, a scientist from Germany, was part of the expedition.

3. The explorers set sail across an icy sea on a Tuesday.

4. Near the Commander Islands, the scientist saw a creature like a giant seal.

5. This sea cow was later named after Steller.

6. Later, on the way back to Siberia, fog forced the ship to land on an island.

7. By May, the crew members were starving.

8. In June of 1742, the survivors found food.

9. The Bering Sea was named in honor of the commander.

B. Proofread the sentences. Write them so that all proper nouns are capitalized.

Example:

I read a book on pandas last saturday.

I read a book on pandas last Saturday.

10. Now I want to go to the zoo on labor day.

11. Giant pandas once lived in many parts of china and tibet.

12. Now they live only in sichuan, in china.

13. About a hundred pandas live in the wolong nature reserve there.

14. Scientists in asia and north america worry that pandas may become extinct.

15. The ministry of forestry is working to save this animal.

16. The world wildlife fund helps, too.

SINGULAR AND PLURAL NOUNS

A. Write the singular nouns in each sentence.

Example:

Many unusual creatures live on the continent of Australia.

continent, Australia

1. The emu is a large flightless bird.
2. The platypus has fur but lays eggs.
3. The echidna looks like a porcupine but eats ants.
4. The kangaroo is a marsupial.
5. A mother carries her helpless baby in her pouch.

B. Write the plural noun or nouns in each sentence.

Example:

Kangaroos live in dry lands.

kangaroos, lands

6. Kangaroos hop on their hind legs.
7. Wallabies and koalas are marsupials.
8. Penguins live on the coast.
9. There are hundreds of lizards.
10. Geckos can walk on ceilings.

C. Write each underlined singular noun. Then write its plural.

Example:

A wild <u>animal</u> lives in Alaska.

animal, animals

11. A <u>wolf</u> howls at the moon.
12. A <u>rabbit</u> runs across a field.
13. A <u>fox</u> is chasing it.
14. A <u>moose</u> shakes its antlers.
15. A bear cub swats at a <u>butterfly</u>.
16. An <u>airplane</u> soars through the sky.
17. It startles a <u>deer</u>.
18. A grizzly bear catches a <u>fish</u>.
19. A <u>mouse</u> makes a <u>home</u> in the wall of a cabin.
20. An <u>eagle</u> dives toward a tree.
21. A <u>squirrel</u> scurries inside a hole.

POSSESSIVE NOUNS

A. Read each sentence, and write each possessive noun.

Example:

A chipmunk took a raisin from my sister's plate.

sister's

1. Some of Colorado's wild animals are not afraid of people.

2. A porcupine chewed my aunt's hat.

3. The blue jays' manners are not very good.

4. One ate part of Grandma's sandwich.

5. Deer eat from our family's garden.

6. My bean plants were a doe's dinner.

7. My father's dream is to have squirrels that don't make any noise.

8. The squirrels' favorite tree is the one beside my bedroom window.

9. I am going to borrow my aunt's camera.

10. I can become America's greatest wildlife photographer.

B. Revise each sentence by replacing the underlined group of words with a word group containing a possessive noun.

Example:

The cat of my friend seems unusually proud.

  My friend's cat

11. The history of that animal is enough to make it proud.

12. People of Egypt tamed wild African cats 2,000 years ago.

13. Before then, cats did not have the role of a pet.

14. The work of the cats was valuable.

15. The problems of the Egyptians with hunger and disease were solved.

16. The cats kept the germs of the rats from spreading.

17. The hunting skill of a feline is good.

18. The appreciation of the pharaohs was great.

SINGULAR AND PLURAL POSSESSIVE NOUNS

A. Write the singular possessive nouns.

Example:
A dog is a human's best friend.

human's

1. A poodle's curly hair makes it cute.
2. My cousin's spaniel is very loyal.
3. Collies are a herder's dream.
4. A shepherd's work is never done.
5. A watchdog's protection helps many.

B. Write the plural possessive nouns.

Example:
People have relied on dogs' talents for at least 12,000 years.

dogs'

6. Many breeds' skills are useful.
7. The hounds' short legs help them.
8. This breed can follow small animals' movements through heavy brush.
9. Huge Saint Bernards have been responsible for some people's rescues.
10. Bloodhounds' keen noses help them hunt for lost hikers.

C. Revise each sentence. Make the underlined words a possessive noun, and underline it.

Example:
Do you like the bright colors
of the toucans?

Do you like the toucans' bright colors?

11. We're learning about the amazing animal life of Costa Rica.

12. The diet of a toucan is fruits, nuts, and insects.

13. You may see the long legs of a crane sticking out of the water.

14. Gulls and pelicans nest on the rocks of the shore.

15. The flights of a bat begin at dusk.

16. Fruit bats and vampire bats live in the forests of the area.

17. The homes of sloths are in the treetops.

18. The slow speed of a sloth makes it easy to spot.

19. The cats of the jungle are jaguars and ocelots.

PRONOUNS

A. Read each sentence, and write the pronoun or pronouns.

Example:

Robin and Paul's garden has many weeds in it.

   it

1. The two of them grow plants.

2. She reads about weeds.

3. He searches through plant catalogs for odd fruits and vegetables.

4. They try to grow them in the garden.

5. "We grow many things," Robin said.

6. "A friend helped us plant popcorn last spring," Paul said.

7. "I will let you try the popcorn later in the afternoon," he said to me.

8. "You should look at the plants," Robin said proudly.

9. "What are they?" I asked.

10. "They are oxeye daisies, the prettiest weeds in the garden!" she said.

B. Revise each sentence. Replace the underlined word or words with a pronoun.

Example:
Jamie Jobb wrote a book titled <u>My Garden</u>.
  Jamie Jobb wrote it.

11. <u>Jamie Jobb</u> wrote the book for ten-year-olds.

12. "<u>My sons and I</u> enjoy gardening," Jamie said.

13. <u>A garden</u> is a good place to learn.

14. A gardener quickly learns about <u>insects</u>.

15. <u>Birds</u> like gardens with fruit trees.

16. <u>Martha Weston</u> drew all the pictures for Jamie Jobb's book.

17. <u>The yellow flowers</u> are daffodils.

18. We bring <u>daffodils</u> to my grandparents each Sunday in spring.

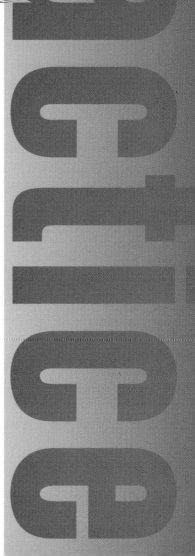

SUBJECT AND OBJECT PRONOUNS

A. Write the subject pronouns.

Example:

We eat potatoes grown in Idaho.
We

1. They came from Henry Spalding.
2. He settled in Idaho in 1836.
3. We believe he brought the first potatoes there.
4. It was this man who gave potatoes to Nez Percé families.
5. They had never seen potatoes.

B. Write the object pronouns.

Example:

Families planted them in the spring.
them

6. Bad weather ruined the crop for them.
7. The next year, a visitor to Spalding's mission wrote about him.
8. This time the Nez Percé had good crops that helped them.
9. A traveler was glad they gave food to her.
10. She made it into a meal.

C. Replace each underlined group of words with a pronoun. Write *subject* or *object* after each pronoun you write.

Example:

Bob and I planted sugar maple trees for my aunt and uncle.

  We—subject

11. The trees will grow to be 100 feet tall.
12. My uncle will tap the trees.
13. My uncle sometimes collects gallons of sap from each tree.
14. He and my aunt will boil it to make syrup.
15. They are going to share it with Bob and me.
16. My aunt buys these trees at the nursery.
17. I learned from my aunt that maple trees have winged seeds.
18. My aunt can identify all thirteen species of maple trees in the United States.

POSSESSIVE PRONOUNS

A. Read the sentences, and write each possessive pronoun.

Example:

"My office is near the ocean," Aunt Shirlene explained.

My

1. My aunt is our favorite marine biologist.
2. We visited her apartment last year, and then she came to see ours.
3. "Please show us your slides!" we asked.
4. Aunt Shirlene takes photos of manatees with her underwater camera.
5. "I'm studying their habitats," she said.
6. She told us about their huge appetites.
7. A manatee would eat its weight in plants each day if it could.
8. She asked Dad if she could borrow his slide projector.
9. She showed us a slide of a manatee with a scar across its back.
10. "I hope you're more careful with your motorboat than this driver was," said my aunt.

B. Show how you could revise the sentences. Write a possessive pronoun to replace each underlined word or group of words.

Example:

"Mitch, would you lend me Mitch's watch?" Zoila asked.

your

11. "Oh, that's right. Zoila's is broken," Mitch replied.

12. "Did Burt lend you Burt's map?" I asked.

13. "No, Bud and Kay lent me Bud and Kay's," she said.

14. She was ready for Zoila's hike.

15. "Where did I put Zoila's camera?" Zoila exclaimed.

16. "You put it in Zoila's backpack," Mitch said.

17. She shook Mitch's and my hands.

18. "Thanks for Mitch's watch," she told Mitch.

19. "How is the camera's battery?" I asked.

ADJECTIVES AND ARTICLES

A. Write the adjectives in these sentences. (Do not write the articles.)

Example:

Their red tomatoes are big!

red, big

1. Martin collects old postcards of giant vegetables.
2. The carrots are long and fat.
3. If someone cut into one onion, a thousand people would cry huge tears!
4. You could make jam for an army from a gigantic strawberry!
5. Paul Bunyan might slip on the peel of a monstrous banana!

B. Write the articles in these sentences.

6. A farmer unloads a huge orange pumpkin.
7. One gourd weighs an amazing amount!
8. A woman from Gresham, Oregon, thrills the crowd with her golden giant.
9. The winner weighs 706 pounds!
10. The pumpkin contest is a success.

C. Revise the sentences. Replace each underlined word with an adjective that is more descriptive. You may need to change the article, too.

Example:

The people at the state fair are a <u>special</u> group.

The people at the state fair are an extraordinary group.

11. The vegetables there were <u>big</u>.
12. The winning pie was <u>good</u>.
13. My ride on the Wheel of Fear was <u>fun</u>.
14. Native Americans performed an <u>old</u> dance.
15. A <u>neat</u> woman taught me about quilts.
16. A band played <u>nice</u> music in a tent.
17. A storyteller told an <u>interesting</u> story.
18. A <u>loud</u> pig escaped from the livestock area.
19. It led dozens of people on a <u>big</u> chase.
20. Finally, its <u>tired</u> owner caught it.

ADJECTIVES THAT COMPARE: -ER, -EST

A. Read each sentence, and write the adjective that compares.

Example:

Bill's plant has the longest vines I've ever seen!

longest

1. His family had the prettier of our two yards.
2. Now the world's largest vine has taken over.
3. Margie Susuki's nicest ball got lost.
4. Bill and Margie searched in their oldest clothes.
5. The yard is denser than a jungle!
6. Margie got tangled in the longest vines.
7. When she tried to move, they got even tighter.
8. Bill went to the largest hardware store in town.
9. He bought the sharpest clippers.
10. The yard is much cleaner without that odd plant!

B. Revise each sentence. Change the underlined adjective so that it compares two things or more than two things. You may need to change or add other words, too.

Example:

Those pumpkins grew <u>fast</u>.

Those pumpkins grew faster than mine.

11. Ralph bought his seeds at a <u>large</u> garage sale.

12. The package had <u>odd</u> instructions.

13. His pumpkin plants turned out <u>weird</u>.

14. Their leaves were <u>strong</u>.

15. Their habit of swatting flies made Ralph <u>happy</u>.

16. The pumpkins could also make <u>high</u> jumps.

17. The pumpkins' skin had a <u>dull</u> color.

18. The neighborhood children have a <u>neat</u> attraction right in their backyard!

ADJECTIVES THAT COMPARE: *MORE, MOST*

A. Write each adjective that compares.

Example:

That is the most unusual plant of all.

most unusual

1. It thought socks were the most wonderful thing it ever tasted.
2. Karen could think of things more delicious than socks.
3. The most helpful plant would eat her brother's tuba.
4. A television-eating plant is more useful.
5. Maybe the plant would swallow her sister's most disgusting perfume.
6. Karen could not think of anything more fun to watch!
7. She found the most beautiful plant book.
8. The information was the most boring she had read, though.
9. The plant itself was more interesting!
10. A biologist would be most fascinated.

B. Revise the sentences to add *more* or *most* to each underlined adjective. You may need to add other words, too.

Example:
Natural wonders are <u>valuable</u>.

Natural wonders are more valuable than all the money in the world.

11. The history of our river is an <u>interesting</u> tale.
12. Long ago, the river was <u>beautiful</u>.
13. The water made the nearby land <u>gorgeous</u>.
14. That area had <u>colorful</u> plant life.
15. Wild animals had <u>outstanding</u> drinking water.
16. Seeing badgers come to the water's edge was <u>exciting</u>.
17. Returning the polluted river to a more natural state was <u>difficult</u>.
18. The restoration has been <u>amazing</u>!
19. The change has helped make the earth an <u>attractive</u> place.

SPECIAL FORMS FOR COMPARING

A. Read the sentences, and write each form of the words *good* and *bad*.

Example:

Doing something fun can help you feel better.

  better

1. My best friend moved away.
2. Then, last week I caught a bad cold.
3. I felt worse each day.
4. I thought this was going to be the worst summer vacation ever!
5. My friend Geri said that reading a book would help me feel better.
6. She said that *The Incredible Journey* is a good book.
7. It's the best book I've read!
8. Geri and I began making our own wilderness book, and I felt better.
9. Geri is good at writing.
10. I'm a better artist, though.

B. Read each sentence, and choose the correct word in parentheses.

Example:
Your celery stalk is the (better, best) of all the food puppets.

best

11. Making talking vegetable puppets was the (worstest, worst) idea I ever had.

12. I was much (worse, worst) than my classmates at making puppets.

13. Then I became (better, gooder) at it.

14. John's carrot looked much (worse, worser) than mine.

15. Suno said her tomato was the (worse, worst) puppet.

16. Her eggplant puppet will look much (better, best).

17. The (best, goodest) puppets are usually not the most realistic.

18. Sasha's new broccoli puppet is (better, best) than his last one because it's brighter.

19. The (bestest, best) part is giving the show.

VERBS

A. Read each sentence, and write the verb.

Example:

Nine planets revolve around our sun.

   revolve

1. Pluto is the planet farthest from the sun.
2. It circles the sun every 248 years.
3. Its temperature drops below −350°F.
4. Pluto was unknown to scientists 100 years ago.
5. Percival Lowell estimated the location of the planet in 1915.
6. He never found the planet.
7. In 1930, Clyde Tombaugh studied the sky with a powerful telescope.
8. He took many photographs through the telescope.
9. Three of his photographs showed a distant planet.
10. In 1978, astronomers discovered a satellite of Pluto.

B. Write the complete predicate of each sentence. Underline the verb.

Example:
Astronomers study the planets and the stars.

 study the planets and the stars

11. Stephen Hawking is a famous astronomer.
12. He studies mysteries of the universe.
13. Black holes seem strange to many of us.
14. These objects are invisible.
15. The gravity of black holes is very strong.
16. Black holes pull nearby comets and planets inside them.
17. Light from nearby stars disappears into black holes, too.
18. Astronomers found these strange holes for the first time about twenty-five years ago.

ACTION VERBS

A. Read each sentence, and write the action verb.

Example:

The alarm rang at 5 A.M.

rang

1. Vanetta jumped out of bed.
2. She dressed herself quickly.
3. Then she helped her mother with breakfast.
4. Vanetta poured the cereal.
5. Vanetta and her mother drove away from their house before dawn.
6. They headed straight for the space shuttle launch site.
7. Vanetta's mother parked in a public viewing area.
8. Vanetta spotted the shuttle's giant fuel tank.
9. The radio announcer reported the launch countdown.
10. The space shuttle *Discovery* rose swiftly.

B. Replace the underlined verb in each sentence with a stronger action verb.

Example:
The movie audience <u>looked</u> at the planet's weird landscape.

   stared

11. A volcano <u>put</u> fiery rocks into the sky.

12. Captain Wong <u>moved</u> away on her space scooter.

13. Boulders <u>came</u> down all around her.

14. The captain <u>spoke</u> loudly into her wrist telephone.

15. Suddenly, a giant lizard <u>came</u> out from behind a rock!

16. With a snarl, it <u>went</u> toward her.

17. Captain Wong <u>took</u> her camera.

18. Despite the danger, she <u>made</u> several photographs.

19. Then she <u>drove</u> away.

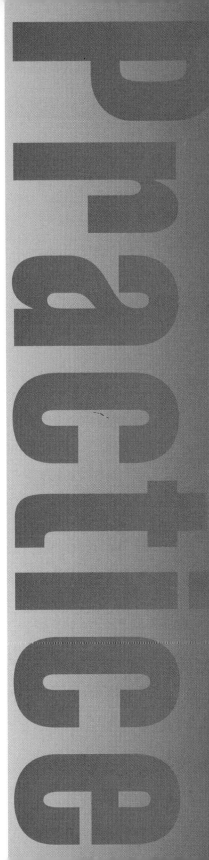

LINKING VERBS

A. Read each sentence, and write the linking verb.

Example:

A UFO is an unidentified flying object.

  is

1. Today the sky seems unusually dark.
2. The air feels still and heavy.
3. Two space creatures are in our backyard!
4. Each creature is rather short.
5. The creatures' hands and feet are green and rubbery.
6. One's voice seems oddly familiar.
7. I am not afraid of these space aliens.
8. The two creatures are my little brother Max and his friend Dillon.
9. They are in their costumes.
10. Max and Dillon became space aliens for a neighborhood play.

B. Write the verb in each sentence. Then tell whether it is a linking verb or an action verb.

Example:

A balloon is a bag full of air.

  is—linking verb

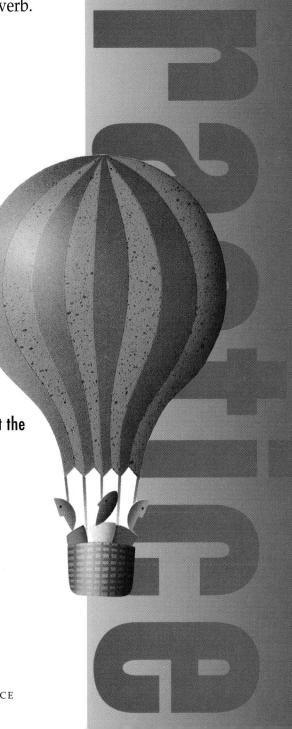

11. Many hot-air balloons are colorful.
12. Our balloon is orange and green.
13. At first my friend and I felt afraid.
14. The pilot spoke kindly to us.
15. She became an expert balloonist several years ago.
16. A gas jet heats the air in the balloon.
17. Now we are high over the valley.
18. The morning air seems very still.
19. The balloon rises toward the clouds.
20. The history of ballooning is interesting.
21. The Montgolfier brothers of France built the first hot-air balloon in 1783.

MAIN VERBS

A. Read each sentence, and write the main verb.

Example:

Alicia has collected hundreds of coins.

collected

1. Alicia is sorting the coins in her collection.
2. She has received a box of pennies.
3. Alicia's great-grandfather had collected some of the pennies.
4. He had saved a penny from the year 1794.
5. Alicia has added many coins to the collection.
6. She is putting her oldest dime away.
7. She will display it tomorrow at the hobby show.
8. She has won a blue ribbon before.
9. Alicia's principal and teachers are serving as judges.
10. They will see her collection for the first time.

B. Write the verbs in each sentence. Underline the main verb.

Example:

An old sea chest has disappeared from the Bankston Museum.

has <u>disappeared</u>

11. The police are finding no clues.
12. They have asked a young detective for help.
13. Hector Fernandez is becoming famous.
14. He has solved eight cases already this year.
15. His parents have set one rule for their son.
16. He will do schoolwork before detective work.
17. This Saturday, Hector Fernandez will solve six long-division problems.
18. Then he will visit the Tidy Attic Antique Store.
19. Hector Fernandez will find the answer to another mystery!

HELPING VERBS

A. Read each sentence, and write the helping verb.

Example:

Shana is always discovering something brand-new.

is

1. Today she is watching ants.
2. She had stared at something all morning.
3. The ants have carried sand all the way across the ant farm.
4. They will lift loads bigger than themselves.
5. That load will be too heavy for the ant!
6. Shana and I are counting ants quickly.
7. How many were living in one place?
8. Shana's questions are making her curious.
9. We will find some answers.
10. I am looking in the encyclopedia!

B. Write the verbs in each sentence. Underline the helping verb.

Example:
Many famous authors have written mysteries.

have written

11. Carl is writing a mystery, too.

12. He will plan his story carefully.

13. Someone in his story has hidden a chest.

14. Someone else had looked for clues.

15. Who will be the mystery person?

16. Carl is keeping a plan in mind.

17. He was listing details about the story events.

18. He is using some of these as clues.

19. He will keep other details secret.

20. He has also created an interesting main character.

21. Carl had chosen a young person as his detective.

22. This character will solve the mystery.

PRESENT TENSE

A. Read each sentence, and write the verb or verbs in the present tense.

Example:

Mrs. Frisby needs help.

needs

1. I like the book *Mrs. Frisby and the Rats of NIMH.*
2. Rats become very intelligent as part of an experiment.
3. Scientists study the rats, and they learn more about the mysteries of intelligence.
4. The rats grow very smart, and they escape from their cages.
5. They run away to the countryside.
6. The rats study agriculture.
7. They want their own farm.
8. Mrs. Frisby, a mouse, needs the rats' help with a problem.
9. The rats have fond memories of her late husband.
10. This book won the John Newbery Medal, and it is my favorite.

B. Write the correct present-tense form of the verb in parentheses ( ).

Example:

Frank (help) vacationers.

   helps

11. He (operate) a small fishing boat.
12. The boat (carry) people out onto the lakes.
13. It (travel) through small canals from one lake to the other.
14. The fishing boat (stop) often.
15. People (board) the boat outside Frank's tackle shop.
16. Frank (raise) his own bait.
17. At the sound of a car horn, Frank (look) around.
18. He always (greet) fishers with a smile.
19. He (like) to tell stories about "the one that got away."
20. Then he (help) the guests bait their hooks and cast their lines.

PAST TENSE

A. Write each verb that is in the past tense.

Example:

The mayor handed awards to community helpers.

> *handed*

1. One woman transported elderly people to their doctors' appointments.

2. Another woman cooked for them.

3. An elderly man read books to them.

4. Fourth graders printed letters for people in a nursing home.

5. A young woman conducted a ballet class at a child care center.

6. A woman in a wheelchair guided children on tours of the art museum.

7. A teenager handled errands for people.

8. A husband and wife demonstrated crafts at the county museum.

9. A college student coached the Special Olympics team.

10. The mayor said that community helpers are the true heroes of our time.

B. Revise each sentence. Change the verb from present tense to past tense.

Example:

A boy sails from Norway to America with his family.

A boy sailed from Norway to America with his family.

11. He travels west to California at age 24.

12. He discovers only a little gold.

13. He purchases a farm with the gold.

14. He changes his last name from Tostenson to Thompson.

15. In 1856, he answers a newspaper ad.

16. The government needs a mail carrier for the long, cold winter.

17. Snow closes the trails through the high Sierra Nevada mountains in early October.

18. Thompson crosses the mountains on skis.

19. Miners and mountain families depend on "Snowshoe" Thompson.

IRREGULAR VERBS

A. Choose the correct verb in parentheses to complete each sentence.

Example:

A hiss (come/came) from the darkest corner of the room.

    came

1. "This is the most boring game I've ever (saw/seen)," groaned Walker.

2. "I (have/had) a better game, but I lost it," Shawn whined.

3. The baby-sitter (think/thought) this would be the longest evening ever.

4. "What a waste of time," Walker (say/said).

5. When he (took/takes) a turn, he landed on a lion.

6. The lion (ate/eat) the armchair!

7. Can you guess what it (did/do) next?

8. The lion (run/ran) out the door.

9. It (drove/drive) away in a truck.

10. A tiger (rode/ride) with it.

B. Revise each sentence. Change the verb or verbs to past tense.

Example:

Hobie takes his next turn.

Hobie took his next turn.

11. The box says "An Adventure Game."
12. The game has a funny-looking board.
13. We see a fierce gorilla on square 16.
14. Square 23 has a spooky cave.
15. Ki thinks the bird on square 41 looks angry.
16. Yori says, "What a strange game!"
17. He gives the instructions from the box.
18. A shiny spinner comes with the game.
19. The rules say "for brave players."
20. The game goes quickly.
21. Hobie goes to a square with a bug.
22. Large red ants eat our lunch.
23. Yori says the game is over.

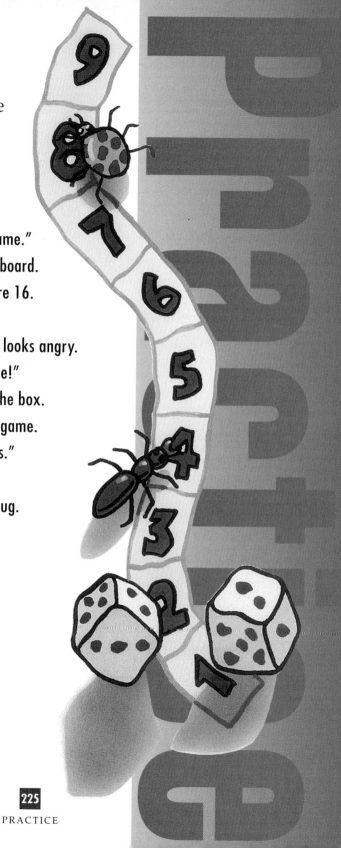

FUTURE TENSE

A. Write the verbs that are in the future tense.

Example:
Tomorrow we will visit one of America's largest cattle ranches.

will visit

1. We will fly over the ocean for hours.
2. Our airplane will land on the slope of a volcano.
3. Then we will ride horses.
4. Instead of beef jerky, we will sample *see moi,* salty Chinese plums.
5. The cowhands on the ranch will call themselves *paniolos.*
6. Our tour of Parker Ranch will stretch across many miles of the big island of Hawaii.
7. We will learn about the history of ranching in the Hawaiian Islands.
8. In the afternoon, we will listen to a talk about King Kamehameha the Great.
9. We will see the remains of the king's home at Kailua tomorrow morning.
10. After that we will head home.

B. Revise each sentence. Change the verb to the future tense.

Example:

The temperature falls rapidly.

The temperature will fall rapidly.

11. A blanket of cold air settles on the valley.

12. Ms. Asato reads the weather data on her computer.

13. She records a warning on a telephone answering machine.

14. Hundreds of fruit and nut growers call the line.

15. Frost damages young plants and buds on trees.

16. The growers work late into the night.

17. They roll their huge wind machines into the orchards.

18. These giant fans move the air.

19. The movement of the air raises temperatures a few degrees.

20. Wet ground also keeps temperatures higher.

ADVERBS

A. Write the adverb in each sentence.

Example:

Settlers waited impatiently at the borders of central Oklahoma.

impatiently

1. At noon on April 22, 1889, the starting guns sounded loudly.

2. The land rush had officially begun.

3. Some settlers rode swiftly.

4. A few of the poorest people ran desperately across the plains.

5. The first settler on each piece of land owned it legally.

6. The swiftest riders quickly reached the lands of their choice.

7. Buggies stopped and hopeful families climbed down.

8. Many lands were already occupied.

9. These settlers had sneaked across.

10. The courts later denied the claims of some of these "Sooners."

B. Choose the correct word in parentheses to complete each sentence.

Example:

Our cows chew (happy/happily).

　happily

11. If corn is (proper/properly) prepared, it makes good winter food for animals.

12. Farm families wait (patiently/patient) for corn to ripen.

13. They work (swift/swiftly) to cut down the stalks.

14. They (careful/carefully) bundle the corn.

15. The wagon full of corn squeaks (noisily/noisy) along.

16. They line a pit (complete/completely) with stones.

17. They work (steady/steadily) to fill it.

18. Then they tramp on the chopped corn (vigorously/vigorous) for a long time.

ADVERBS THAT COMPARE

A. Read each sentence, and write the adverb that compares. Remember to include the word *more* or *most* when it is used.

Example:

Hard coal burns more brightly than soft coal.

more brightly

1. The Bielski family huddled closer.
2. The temperature had dropped faster than anyone could remember.
3. Stan looked the hardest to find wood.
4. Mr. Bielski had driven the farthest of anyone to try to find a job.
5. He wrote letters more desperately in winter.
6. Someone knocked louder than a jackhammer on the family's front door.
7. It had frozen harder than ice.
8. They smiled to see Aunt Gail, with Stan grinning the most happily.
9. Mike made the fire burn more briskly.
10. Then Aunt Gail unpacked ham, and Stan ate the most hungrily of all.

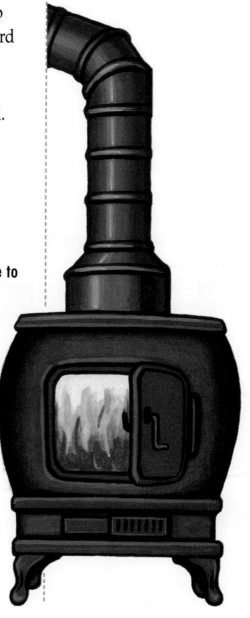

B. Choose the correct word or words in parentheses.

Example:

The coal-mining song sung (more frequently/most frequently) of all is "John Henry."

  most frequently

11. A real miner named John Henry swung his hammer (powerfuller/more powerfully) than any other miner.

12. He drove the steel bar (deeper/deepest) into the coal than his partner drove it.

13. Some say he worked the (hard/hardest) of all the coal miners in West Virginia.

14. The owners wanted to make money (more quickly/most quickly) than anyone else.

15. A steam drill would drill holes (rapid/more rapidly) than a miner.

16. John Henry said, "I can drive steel (faster/fastest) than that steam drill!"

17. The next day he pounded the steel (farther/farthest) than the steam drill!

NEGATIVES

A. Read each sentence, and write the negative. Write the two words that make up any contraction you find.

Example:

The Plateau people didn't copy the art of the Northwest Coast people.

didn't—did not

1. Most never carved totem poles.
2. They didn't stay in one place.
3. There isn't any reason to visit berry patches in the springtime.
4. No berries are ripe then.
5. During winter, hunters can't hunt easily in the snowy mountains.
6. Dried salmon doesn't spoil, so the Plateau people dried salmon.
7. Nobody thought winter was a sensible time to travel.
8. Plateau people went nowhere then.
9. Winds did nothing to their log houses.
10. Their summer homes weren't as sturdy as the log houses.

B. Revise each sentence so it becomes a negative statement. You may change any words you need to change.

Example:

My sister and I had an easy time making a totem pole.

My sister and I didn't have an easy time making a totem pole.

11. We found some large cedar trees.
12. We received permission to cut one down.
13. We had cut down a large tree before.
14. Someone helped us move the tree.
15. We were allowed to use my father's tools.
16. My mother let us use her paints.
17. Our first drawing was very good.
18. The eagle looked like an eagle.
19. The bear seemed fierce.
20. The work went very fast.
21. Our totem pole looked exactly like the picture we had drawn.
22. Our totem pole is very tall.
23. We are very pleased with it.
24. My mother asked us to leave it up.
25. She wants everyone to see it.

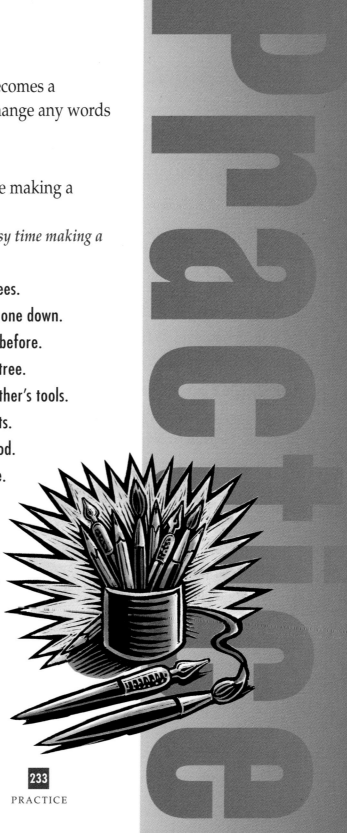

A. Choose the word in parentheses that correctly completes each sentence.

Example:

Laura had a snack before she went (too/to/two) bed.

to

1. First, she ate (too/to/two) bananas.
2. Then she went (too/to/two) the bread box.
3. She found (too/to/two) slices of bread inside.
4. She ate a pickle, (too/to/two).
5. She was on her way (too/to/two) bed when she heard a popping sound.
6. Pa had become hungry, (too/to/two).
7. The (too/to/two) of them ate popcorn.
8. Then Laura went (too/to/two) her room.
9. She was (too/to/two) full to sleep.
10. She read (too/to/two) stories by candlelight before falling asleep.

B. Proofread these sentences. Rewrite correctly each sentence in which *too*, *to*, or *two* is used incorrectly.

Example:

To birds circle above the prairie.

Two birds circle above the prairie.

11. A weak deer falls too its knees.

12. It can barely walk two the water hole.

13. In to hours, it gets its strength back.

14. Every region has grazing animals, browsing animals, and hunting animals, to.

15. A vulture has to sharp eyes.

16. When one vulture glides down, too or three others will usually follow.

17. Two familiar species in America are the turkey vulture and the black vulture.

18. One vulture is close too extinction.

19. The California condor was once a familiar sight two Native Americans.

20. They gave the name *thunderbird* to the condor.

GOOD, WELL

A. Write the word in parentheses that correctly completes each sentence.

Example:

"This lagoon is a (good/well) place to watch fish," said Linda.

good

1. "These fins should fit you (good/well)," she told Joe.
2. "I can swim (good/well)," he said.
3. "It's still a (good/well) idea to wear a life jacket," she told him.
4. "If you swallow water, you won't be able to swim (good/well)."
5. Linda found a (good/well) mask.
6. Joe could see (good/well) underwater.
7. He got a (good/well) look at fish.
8. "That one is a (good/well) clown!" said Joe.
9. He was (good/well) at using his snorkel.
10. Later, he ate a (good/well) meal.

B. Proofread these sentences. Rewrite correctly each sentence in which *good* or *well* is used incorrectly.

Example:

My father taught me to tie flies good.

My father taught me to tie flies well.

11. Lake Slo was a well fishing spot.
12. It is a good spot if you're a fish!
13. None of the six of us had well luck.
14. I thought I'd do good because I'd brought thirty of my best flies.
15. "What good flies!" said Aunt Sandra.
16. "How did you do that so good?"
17. "Dad taught me to use good materials," I replied.
18. It's not a well idea to be in the hot sun all day without a hat.
19. The hot dogs we ate for dinner were good.
20. Laverne said, "You did very good today."

THEY'RE, THEIR, THERE

A. Write the word *they're, their,* or *there* to complete each sentence correctly.

Example:

On the banks of the Jumna River, workers called *dhobis* are doing _____ daily work.

  their

1. _____ washing clothes for the people of Delhi, India.

2. They wash clothes on the rocks _____.

3. The dhobis don't earn much, but _____ proud of their work.

4. Many of _____ parents were dhobis.

5. Now _____ worried about pollution.

6. _____ are many factories along the Jumna River.

7. Some pour _____ waste into the river.

8. No matter how hard the dhobis work, _____ not able to get clothes clean.

9. Stronger laws against pollution would keep the river cleaner _____.

10. Then the dhobis could make _____ customers happy again.

B. Proofread these sentences. Rewrite correctly each sentence in which *they're, their,* or *there* is used incorrectly.

Example:
Why are the fourth graders wearing gloves on there hands?

Why are the fourth graders wearing gloves on their hands?

11. Their helping to recycle trash.

12. Students sort they're lunch trash.

13. Paper goes in the can over their.

14. Many students bring there lunches in lunch boxes.

15. Their saving trees.

16. A few students are carrying buckets of food scraps in their hands.

17. They're taking them to the compost pile.

18. They're teacher has helped them learn how to turn garbage into a kind of fertilizer.

19. They have they're own garden section.

20. Their growing tomatoes and corn.

IT'S, ITS

A. Write the word *it's* or *its* to complete each sentence correctly.

Example:

The carp family makes (it's, its) home on four different continents.

its

1. (It's/Its) the largest fish family.

2. (It's/Its) best-known member is the goldfish.

3. A carp has no teeth in (it's/its) jaws.

4. It grinds up (it's/its) food with special teeth in its throat.

5. (It's/Its) a peaceful fish, though.

6. A carp prefers warm, slow-moving water for (it's/its) home.

7. (It's/Its) main food is weeds.

8. In Japan, (it's/its) common to see large, beautiful carp in ponds.

9. A carp in a pond must be protected from (it's/its) natural enemies.

10. (It's/Its) not unusual for large carp to live fifty years or more!

B. Proofread these sentences. Rewrite correctly each sentence in which *it's* or *its* is used incorrectly.

Example:

The train puts on it's lights.

> *The train puts on its lights.*

11. Its beginning to get dark.
12. It's engine hums as the train speeds up the hill.
13. The train carries fifty travelers in its passenger cars.
14. It's dining car is near the caboose.
15. The passengers get off the train at its next stop.
16. Its hard work to unload the luggage.
17. Another train arrives with its' lights on.
18. Its driver has followed the last train.
19. It's clear this is a wilderness train.
20. It's passengers are on a trip through the Rockies.

YOU'RE, YOUR

A. Write the word *you're* or *your* to complete each sentence correctly.

Example:

"You said (you're, your) uncle is a farmer," Masanori said to Van.

your

1. "(You're/Your) right," said Van.

2. "(You're/Your) kidding!" he said.

3. "(You're/Your) uncle's land is underwater!" Masanori continued.

4. "Did you bring (you're/your) fishing pole?" asked Van.

5. "Yes, it's in the back of (you're/your) uncle's car," said Masanori.

6. "(You're/Your) catching dinner," said Van.

7. "(You're/Your) giving me a hint," replied Masanori.

8. Then he exclaimed, "(You're/Your) uncle must be a catfish farmer!"

9. "I know that (you're/your) fond of fish," Van said.

10. "(You're/Your) a true friend for inviting me here," said Masanori.

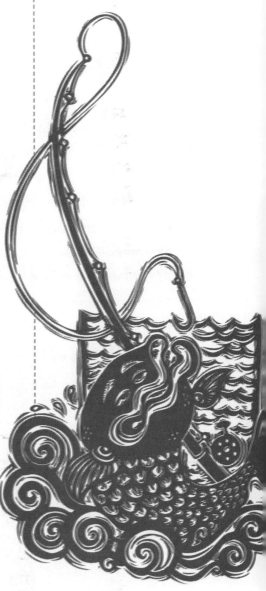

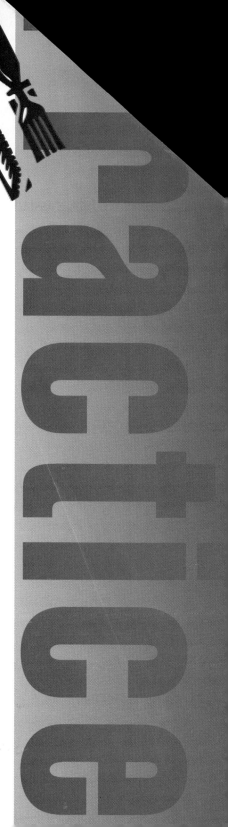

B. Proofread these sentences. Rewrite correctly each sentence in which *you're* or *your* is used incorrectly.

Example:

You're Thanksgiving dinner is almost ready.

Your Thanksgiving dinner is almost ready.

11. I hear you're aunt made the gravy.

12. I hope you're appetite is good.

13. Your having the biggest turkey I've ever seen!

14. Your Thanksgiving dinners are always a treat.

15. Where are you're plates for setting the table?

16. I'm glad your inviting the neighbors for dinner, too.

17. Your going to enjoy the salad I'm making.

18. Is it true that your serving fish, too?

19. I think you're going to have the best Thanksgiving ever.

OMMA

d commas where

plateaus and a
beautiful waterfall.

Zimbabwe has grasslands, plateaus, and a
beautiful waterfall.

1. Harare Bulawayo and Nyala are three of its cities.

2. Zimbabwe's four neighbors are Mozambique Zambia Botswana and South Africa.

3. The Ndebele the Shana the Shanga and the Botanga are the main peoples.

4. Zimbabwe has many national parks botanical gardens and recreation areas.

5. Animals birds and fish are protected.

6. Elephants lions and buffalos are common.

7. Cheetahs hippos and rhinos live there.

8. The most common antelopes are the impala the waterbuck and the greater kudu.

9. Three rare antelopes are the eland the nyala and the klipspringer.

10. In Hwange National Park you may see a giraffe a hyena and a wildebeest.

B. Proofread these sentences. Rewrite them, putting commas in the right places.

Example:

The green mamba snake is beautiful swift and deadly.

The green mamba snake is beautiful, swift, and deadly.

11. Mambas eat lizards rodents and birds.
12. The green mamba has lime-green skin a long head and a large mouth.
13. Pythons eat rodents lizards and small mammals.
14. They live in Africa Asia and Australia.
15. They attack grab and squeeze their prey.
16. The ball python is a short strong and handsome snake.
17. It eats rats mice and other rodents.
18. The African rock python has black yellow and brown markings.
19. These snakes live in south Africa east Africa north Africa and Arabia.
20. Poisonous snakes include cobras vipers and rattlesnakes.
21. These snakes are colorful helpful and dangerous.

COMMAS AFTER INTRODUCTORY WORDS AND IN DIRECT ADDRESS

A. Write the sentences. Insert commas in the correct places.

Example:

"Well you are just a servant!"

"Well, you are just a servant!"

1. "Yes we are going to the ball," said the stepsister to Cinderella.
2. "No you may not go along," she said.
3. "Yes I will scrub the floors."
4. "Well you couldn't go in that, anyway!"
5. "Well our elegant carriage is ready!"

B. Write the sentences, using commas to set off words in direct address.

6. "Mom Cinderella didn't mend my dress!"
7. "There's someone outside Cinderella!"
8. "Welcome our visitor girls!"
9. "Sir I'm sure my foot will fit that slipper."
10. "Young lady I'd like you to try, too," the prince said to Cinderella.

C. Proofread these sentences. Rewrite them so the commas are in the correct places.

Example:
"Yes our sister, wed the prince."
"Yes, our sister wed the prince."

11. "No we're, not jealous!" said one stepsister.

12. "Sir we, wish her a happy life."

13. "Sister please show this gentleman, to the door!" she continued.

14. "Mom it isn't, fair!" they wailed.

15. "Well let's, just have supper and forget about it."

16. "Yes that's a good, idea!" they said.

17. "Darlings where did you, put my recipe book?" the mother asked.

18. "Here, it is Mother!" they said.

19. "Turn, to the apple recipes dear."

20. "Well someone used up, the apples!"

21. "Yes I fed them to, the dog this morning!" giggled the younger girl.

22. "Well perhaps Cinderella will let us, visit her in the palace."

ADDITIONAL PRACTICE

DIALOGUE AND DIRECT QUOTATIONS

A. Write the words spoken directly by a character.

Example:

"Did you see the game?" Susan asked.
  "Did you see the game?"

1. "I watched the Tigers," said Alan.
2. "I don't mean major league baseball," Susan said.
3. "I mean the Little League World Series," she said.
4. "Who was playing?" Alan asked.
5. "Panama and Long Beach played," Susan said.

B. Rewrite the sentences. Add quotation marks.

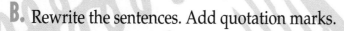

Example:

It was exciting, she said.
  "It was exciting," she said.

6. Alan asked, Who were you for?
7. Susan said, I was for Panama.
8. Did they win? asked Alan.
9. Long Beach won, Susan replied.
10. They won twice in a row! she exclaimed.

C. Proofread these sentences. Rewrite them with each direct quotation correctly set off in quotation marks.

Example:

"Who's the best ball player? asked Jan.

"Who's the best ball player?" asked Jan.

11. "Henry Aaron hit the most home runs in major league history, said Walt."

12. How many did he hit?" she asked.

13. "Walt said, I think he hit 755."

14. You're right, Walt, she said.

15. "I thought it was Babe Ruth, said Elena.

16. Ruth was second," Mrs. Tillman replied."

17. "Have you heard of Josh Gibson? she asked.

18. "He was in the Negro League, said Steve."

19. He may have hit 900 home runs," he added."

20. "What about Sadaharu Oh? asked Jan.

21. "He was Japan's greatest power hitter, she said.

22. "How many home runs did he hit? asked Steve.

23. I know it's over 800, Jan replied."

24. Walt said, "The exact number is 868.

25. "I found it in this book, he said."

TITLES

A. Write each title correctly.

Example:

Waymon is reading the book Feathers Like a Rainbow to his younger brother.

Feathers Like a Rainbow

1. Waymon learned about South America by reading the magazine Skipping Stones.

2. When he was younger, he loved the book is your mama a llama?

3. He is learning to play a song from Brazil called Wave.

4. His favorite folktale is a South American story called Josecito the Goat.

5. Waymon just got the magazine Animals.

6. The title of one story is Spectacled Bears of South America.

7. He read about crocodiles in the book reptiles of the world.

8. He likes the poem Crocodile's Toothache.

9. The song Boa Constrictor also makes him laugh.

10. When he saw the movie The Land Before Time, he thought of the rain forest.

B. Rewrite these sentences so that the titles are written correctly.

Example:

Ike has read the book Justin Morgan Had a Horse three times.

> Ike has read the book *Justin Morgan Had a Horse* three times.

11. His favorite song is "stewball."

12. He also sings Strawberry Roan.

13. When he was little, his favorite poem was "ride away, ride away."

14. His favorite movie is The Black Stallion.

15. He knows the poem Paul Revere's Ride.

16. Ike got the book "smoky the cowhorse."

17. He will read it as soon as he finishes berchick, my Mother's horse.

18. He plans to read the book Sky Dogs.

19. National Velvet is a movie about children who train a horse.

20. Ike also likes the movie "the man from Snowy River."

21. The magazine National Geographic had an article on wild horses.

22. Sometimes Ike finds articles about horses in the magazine Ranger rick.

23. He did a report on the book Training a Colt.

ABBREVIATIONS

A. For each group of words, choose the abbreviation that is written correctly.

Example:

(Febr./Feb.) 1

Feb.

1. (Dr./Doc.) Han
2. Elm (St./Str.)
3. (Unit. St./U.S.) mail
4. (Mstr./Mr.) Kaiser
5. (Ms./Mss.) Lisa Andrews
6. Second (Av./Ave.)
7. (Snt./St.) Patrick's Day
8. (Aug./Agt.) 29
9. 25 Oak (Ro./Rd.)
10. (Tue./Tues.), July 3

B. Write each underlined word or group of words as an abbreviation.

Example:

Take North Meridian <u>Road</u> to Will Rogers World Airport.

Rd.

11. My family is visiting Oklahoma in <u>December</u>.

12. Last <u>Sunday</u> I read a book about Will Rogers.

13. My teacher, <u>Doctor</u> Moore, loaned it to me.

14. I picked it up at her house on <u>East Summerlin Avenue</u>.

15. <u>William Penn</u> Rogers was born in Indian Territory, which is now Oklahoma.

16. <u>Mister</u> and Mrs. Rogers were Cherokee.

17. After working as a cowhand in the <u>United States</u>, Will went to Argentina and <u>worked</u> as a gaucho.

18. Rogers later made comedy films that many Americans watched every <u>Saturday</u> night.

Note: Italic page numbers in main headings refer to additional practice.